KNITTING

MOCHIMOCHI

KNITTING
MOCHIMOCHI

20
SUPER-CUTE
STRANGE DESIGNS
for Knitted
Amigurumi

ANNA HRACHOVEC

PHOTOGRAPHS BY BRANDI SIMONS

WATSON-GUPTILL PUBLICATIONS / NEW YORK

Published in the United States by Watson-Guptill Publications, an imprint of the Crown Publishing Group, a division of Random House, Inc., New York

www.crownpublishing.com
www.watsonguptill.com

WATSON GUPTILL is a registered trademark and the WG and Horse designs are trademarks of Random House, Inc.

Photographs on the following pages copyright © 2010 to Brandi Simons: 1–13, 22 bottom right, 24 bottom right, 28 bottom, 35 bottom right, 38 bottom, 39 bottom right, 43–49, 51–59. 61–63, 65 bottom, 66–72, 76–77, 79 bottom, 80–81, 83 bottom, 84–85, 88–91, 93 bottom, 94–95, 97 bottom, 98–99, 102–103, 105–107, 111–114, 115 bottom, 116–121, 122 bottom, 123 top and bottom, 124 bottom, 125–127. All other photographs copyright © 2010 by Anna Hrachovec.

Library of Congress Cataloging-in-Publication Data

Hrachovec, Anna.
Knitting mochimochi : 20 super cute strange designs for knitted amigurumi toys / Anna Hrachovec.
p. cm.
Includes index.
ISBN 978-0-8230-2664-7
1. Amigurumi—Patterns. 2. Soft toy making. I. Title.
TT829.H73 2010
745.592'4—dc22   2009037073

Designed by Laura Palese

ISBN: 978-0-8230-2664-7

Printed in China

First Printing, 2010

3 4 5 6 7 8 9 / 18 17 16 15 14 13 12 11 10

FOR JOHN

ACKNOWLEDGMENTS

I am grateful for the many people who contributed their talents, enthusiasm, and hard work to make this book possible. Many thanks to **my husband John** for his day-to-day support and his confidence in my silly toys, and to **my mother-in-law Bonney,** who inspired me to take up knitting again. Her crafting energy puts mine to shame.

The photography in this book was a team effort of friends and family. I couldn't have worked with a better photographer than **Brandi,** who was generous with her time and creativity, and who even sometimes risked injury to get the perfect shot. Her family's friendship made the photography process an adventure instead of a headache.

My parents and **our friends in Oklahoma** always came through with the perfect props, locations, and modeling to visualize a world in which toys live harmoniously with people. Thank you to **Rick, the Scotts, Ching, Sandi and Serenity Aveda Day Spa, Leah, Geri and Loren, the Rowden family, April, Hannah,** and **Amy and David Simons**. Thank you also to **Yale Avenue Christian Church** and **the Collinsville Fire Department**. (Yes, we even got a fire department involved.)

I love **my pattern testers**! Thank you so much to all of them, especially those who have been helping me from the beginning: **Angela, Joan, Marti, Tracy, Hannah,** and **Miki**. I am blown away when I think of all the hours they have spent carefully reviewing my patterns and making their own versions of my toys, which often end up cuter than the originals.

I am very thankful for the supplies and other help provided by **Rhichard at Koigu Wool Designs** and **Shannon at Cascade Yarns.**

Lastly, my gratitude to everyone at **Watson-Guptill** for making this book happen, especially my editors **Joy Aquilino,** who guided me with patience and good humor, and **Linda Hetzer,** who worked so hard to make this book the best it could possibly be.

CONTENTS

I dutifully knitted scarves and hats for a long time. But one day a few years ago, I started knitting toys on a whim, and now I can't stop!

The first toy I made was knitted flat in a simple shape and sewn up. It looked like an unevenly formed blob. But when I added two eyes with some spare embroidery thread, suddenly the blob came to life and looked back at me. I fell in love with my anthropomorphic blob! We read magazines and watched "Seinfeld" reruns together. I knitted a few more blobs for friends, and my friends fell in love with their blobs, too. Soon, I was hooked, and I started using the technique of knitting in the round to populate my life with more three-dimensional blob-like creatures, such as elephants and bathtubs.

The toys I knit are inspired by everything cute, funny, or strange that I see, starting with the wonderfully bizarre character designs I first found in Japan when I lived there as a high-school exchange student. There is no end to the rampant cuteness in that small island nation—even the food is cute, like **mochi** (MO-chee), a sticky-rice sweet of which I'm a big fan. Early on, I decided to name my toy design company **Mochimochi** after this adorable edible and its squishy texture that reminds me of a soft toy. My love of cute and strange things has led me to "mochify" all manner of animals, objects, and even weather patterns.

From a knitter's perspective, making toys, or **amigurumi** (ah-mee-goo-ROO-mee), as they are often called,

after the Japanese term for knitted or crocheted toys, is great fun. They are quick projects—some take less than an hour to make—and they don't have to fit anyone. Well, there are a couple of exceptions in this book to that second point (see the "Impractical Wearables" section for some examples), but still, you'll never find yourself asking someone, "Does this toy make me look fat?"

Knitting Mochimochi offers a herd of all-new and all-cute toy patterns to knit. The projects are tailored to a variety of skill levels and time commitments, from a one-inch-long hamster to an entire city block. You'll also learn how to design your own toy, from sketch to finish, so you can fall in love with your own primordial blob.

And fear not, beginners! Though many of the projects in this book introduce you to new techniques, there are plenty of instructional photos to help you along, and in the back you'll find an illustrated guide to basic knitting techniques. Plus, unlike a sweater, a slightly lumpy knitted toy is all the more lovable.

So I welcome you to a place where your inner child and inner knitting geek can get together for a play date, a place where pigs wear '60s hairdos and friendly monsters munch on your feet.

Welcome to Mochimochi land!

WHY I KNIT TOYS—AND WHY YOU SHOULD, TOO!

There are three major reasons why I knit toys and reading about them will probably convince you that you, too, were destined to knit toys.

I loved toys as a kid and love them even more as a grownup.

Toys, people! Who doesn't love toys? Everyone could use something silly looking back at them to make them smile. Sure, you could get a pet, but then there's all the mess and feeding and vet bills. A knitted toy doesn't need any shots, just a squeeze once in a while. And there's no need to be embarrassed. In the 21st century—the cutest century to date—you can hug a toy, carry a toy around in your bag, or display a toy on your desk without shame.

I love to knit.

If you are a knitter, you don't need to read this. If you're not a knitter, why aren't you? It's like so totally the best hobby ever. With just basic techniques, you can create soft, snuggly works of art with your own two hands. Plus, like a kitten, you'll get to play with balls of yarn. And millions of kittens can't be wrong.

I ran out of people to knit scarves and hats for.

Scarves and hats are great for crisp autumn days. But what about hot days, or days when you cannot bring yourself to knit yet another scarf for Aunt Mildred's birthday? May I suggest a knitted television, or perhaps a knitted angel and devil that Auntie can wear on her shoulders?

Believe me, Aunt Mildred will thank you. A knitted toy is much more fun to unwrap than a knitted garment or a store-bought toy. You might even say that a knitted toy is an ideal gift. But what if you don't have an Aunt Mildred? Who are all these toys for?

WHOM TO KNIT TOYS FOR: A GUIDE

Each pattern in this book comes with an utterly arbitrary, often silly suggestion of whom to knit the toy for. The truth is, in my experience, there is no one proper recipient of a knitted toy!

It seems anyone is happy to receive a new yarn-and-stuffing friend. I asked readers of my blog to tell me about the recipients of these handmade gifts. Here is a small sample of their responses.

- FATHERS-IN-LAW
- ELECTRICIANS
- SINGLE GALS
- CRIMINAL LAW PROFESSORS
- EX-BOYFRIENDS
- NUTRITIONISTS
- GODDAUGHTERS
- COWORKERS
- EXCHANGE STUDENTS
- NEWLYWEDS
- HOSPITAL PATIENTS
- COUSINS
- CLINICAL PSYCHOLOGISTS
- BABIES
- VEGETARIANS
- GREAT-GRANDMOTHERS

Whether they're friends you love, acquaintances you like, or strangers you want to surprise, everyone deserves a knitted toy, including yourself!

DON'T FORGET BEAUTY QUEENS!

let's get
STARTED

Ready to get started knitting a toy? Of course you are! (I was just asking to be polite.)

Let's go over the "what" and the "how" to get you to "Wow, I made a toy!"

STUFF YOU'LL NEED

YARN

One great thing about knitting toys is that you can use almost any yarn to make them, and most toys are pretty small and don't require too much of it. You can purchase just a skein or two at your local yarn store, or you can raid your own stash and use some yarn you have lying around from a previous project. Yay!

The thickness of your yarn will determine how big your toy is. I usually work with worsted-weight yarn, but I like to use fingering-weight yarn for tiny toys and chunky or bulky yarn for extra big and huggable toys.

Yarn is made from a variety of different fibers, and most of them can be used to knit toys. Here are some of the most common:

Wool

I often knit with wool yarn because I love the way it looks. It is a flexible fiber that is forgiving and easy to work with. You need to take extra care when washing it, but super-wash varieties are less likely to felt and shrink.

Cotton

Another natural fiber, cotton is durable and a little easier to wash than wool. It tends to be less forgiving than wool, but if you're knitting for a child or someone who is allergic to wool, it's a good choice.

Acrylic

Acrylic can be very affordable, durable, and washable, and so it's a great choice for toys that will be used and loved. It can feel kind of scratchy to work with, though, and many people choose not to use it because it is not a natural fiber.

Other fibers and blends

It's fun to experiment with different kinds of yarn, and I've personally never met a yarn I thought shouldn't be used to knit a toy. While they go in and out of fashion for knitted garments, novelty yarns with their interesting colors and textures can add new dimensions and personalities to toys.

YARN WEIGHT SYSTEM

YARN WEIGHT CATEGORIES	TYPES OF YARN IN CATEGORY	KNIT GAUGE RANGE (in Stockinette stitch to 4 inches)	RECOMMENDED NEEDLE SIZES (U.S/metric sizes)
0 LACE	Fingering, 10-count crochet thread	33–40 sts	000–1/1.5–2.25mm
1 SUPER FINE	Sock, fingering, baby	27–32 sts	1 to 3/2.25–3.25mm
2 FINE	Sport, baby	23–26 sts	3 to 5/3.25–3.75mm
3 LIGHT	DK, light worsted	21–24 sts	5 to 7/3.75–4.5mm
4 MEDIUM	Worsted, afghan, aran	16–20 sts	7 to 9/4.5–5.5mm
5 BULKY	Chunky, craft, rug	12–15 sts	9 to 11/5.5–8mm
6 SUPER BULKY	Bulky, roving	6–11 sts	11 and larger/8mm and larger

Adapted from the Standard Yarn Weight System of the Craft Yarn Council of America.

NEEDLES

Types

Straight needles, two long sticks with points on one end, are only good for knitting flat, straight pieces of fabric. That's why I rarely use them when making my three-dimensional toys.

Double-pointed needles, or dpns for short, have a point at each end and are used for circular knitting. They are sold in sets of five needles, but you will usually only use four at a time.

Circular needles are good for projects that involve larger circumferences (more than 60 or so stitches). They can also be used to knit smaller circumferences. See The Magic Loop (page 40) for more information.

Sizes

The most important thing when picking needles is to match your needle size with your yarn. (See gauge on page 19.) Every person knits with a different tension, but when knitting with worsted-weight yarn I use either size 5 US (3.75mm) or 6 US (4.0mm) needles, depending on the type of project. If you think your stitches are too loose, then they probably are, and it's time to move down a needle size. I start with needles a size or two smaller than the recommended needle size. This makes relatively tight stitches, with no big gaps for stuffing to show through.

Lengths

Depending on the circumference of your knitting, you will want to use double-pointed needles that are 5, 6, or 7 inches long. You could, in theory, use 7-inch needles for everything, but if you're working with a small number of stitches, longer needles can be awkward and difficult to use.

Materials

All needles come in a variety of materials. I work with double-pointed needles made of bamboo, because I like that they are lightweight and smooth, but not slippery. Try needles made of aluminum, wood, or plastic to see what works best for you.

STUFFING

Stuffing will turn your toy from a limp piece of knitting into something you can hug or use as an armrest.

Like yarn and needles, stuffing comes in a variety of materials. I prefer to use polyester fiberfill because it's lightweight, springy, and soft.

Wool stuffing is a natural alternative to polyester. It has a denser feel, and you need to use more care to dry it thoroughly if it gets wet. Other natural alternatives include bamboo and corn-based stuffing. Cotton can also be used as a stuffing, but it tends to get lumpy and compacted, so I don't recommend it.

In a pinch, especially for smaller toys, you can also stuff with scraps of yarn.

EYES

Eyes can be made of yarn, buttons, or a variety of other materials.

I use plastic "safety eyes" in most projects in this book. They are very easy to use, but despite their name, they are not safe for children under the age of three. See Childproofing Your Toys (page 42) for more information on alternatives.

My other preference is for eyes embroidered with a few simple stitches in a contrasting-colored yarn. (See page 26.)

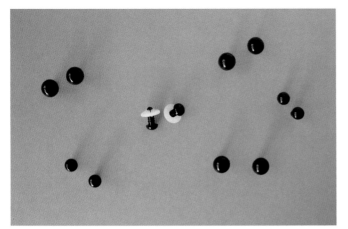

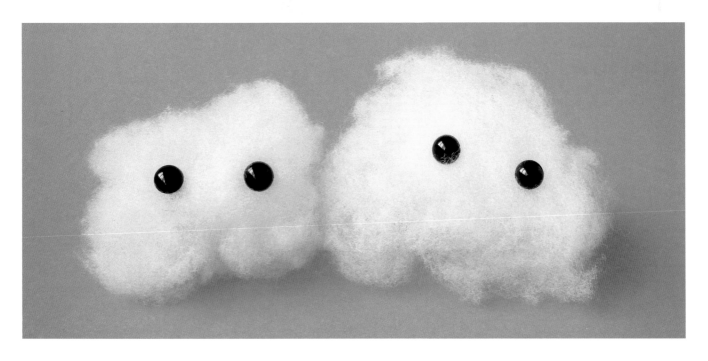

TOOLS

A stitch marker will help you remember where the rounds in your knitting begin and end. Stitch markers come in different varieties, but they're essentially just small rings, so if you don't have store-bought markers, you can make your own by tying pieces of contrasting-colored yarn in small loops.

A tapestry needle looks like a jumbo-size sewing needle. It's used with yarn for seaming, embroidering details, and weaving in loose ends.

Tapestry needles come in different sizes, so you should make sure that you're using one that is big enough to thread your yarn through, but small enough that it will easily slip between your stitches.

A stitch holder allows you to hold live stitches temporarily so that you can come back to them later. You slip your stitches onto the open end, and close it like a safety pin. If you don't have one on hand and you need to hold stitches, you can simply thread a spare piece of yarn through the stitches and tie it shut.

A counter helps you keep track of the row or round that you're on without having to keep it all in your head. The type pictured is an easy-to-use clicking device. Or you can simply make hash marks on a piece of paper.

Scissors of any type will do, but small ones with a pointed tip are easiest to use for knitting projects.

A crochet hook is used for patterns that call for a provisional cast-on. It's also handy for picking up stitches dropped accidentally.

A measuring tape is essential for checking gauge and for customizing a wearable item.

Straight pins are helpful when attaching multiple appendages so you can get the right spacing before you sew them in place.

stitch markers

tapestry needles

counter

stitch holder

scissors

GAUGE: TO CHECK OR NOT TO CHECK?

Checking gauge is boring. Most books will tell you that it's important to check it anyway, by knitting up a swatch of your yarn before beginning to knit a garment, to make sure that it will be the right size when you're finished. That's where toys differ from garments—they don't have to fit over your head, or drape well, or any of that nonsense.

You hereby have my permission to start knitting away with whatever yarn you like, as long as you use a needle size that gives you tight enough stitches so your stuffing won't show through once you've finished. However, skipping gauge-checking means it's likely that your finished toy will be a different size from my finished toy.

There are a few wearable patterns in this book for which I make an exception. I strongly recommend checking the gauge, when I have included it in the pattern. Otherwise, I've made it really simple for you, using just a couple different types of yarn and needle sizes for all of the projects.

Checking gauge takes only a few minutes and a few simple steps:

1. Using the yarn you have chosen for a project and the needles size called for in the pattern, knit a flat square about 5 inches by 5 inches in stockinette stitch (knit on the right side, purl on the wrong side).

2. Lay the square flat without stretching it—it's helpful to pin it to an ironing board or other surface so it won't slip around—and use a ruler or measuring tape to measure how many stitches and how many rows you have per inch.

3. If your stitch/row counts are significantly bigger than in the given gauge, switch to a smaller-size needle and try again.

If your stitch/row counts are significantly smaller than in the given gauge, you have a couple of options. If you can move up a needle size and not end up with gaps between your stitches where your stuffing will show through, then try a larger-size needle. If using a larger needle will produce gaps, then try a thicker yarn or decide that you can live with a smaller-size toy in the end. Especially with the smaller projects, it doesn't hurt to just start knitting and see what you get!

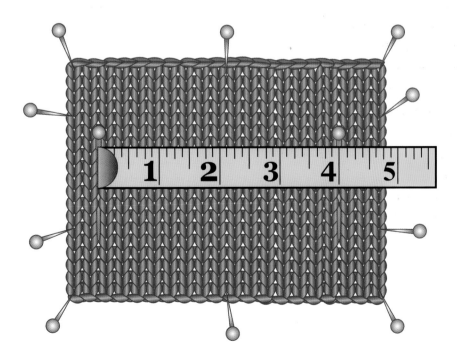

BASIC TOY TECHNIQUES

If you are a beginning knitter, or if you would like to brush up on your techniques, you can refer to the Knitting Essentials on pages 133–140.

THE KNITTING

Using Double-Pointed Needles

Knitting in the round is a great way to make three-dimensional toys with interesting shapes and minimal seaming, and I prefer to use double-pointed needles when knitting the small circumferences of toys. (For using a circular needle, see The Magic Loop on page 40.)

Double-pointed needles look much scarier than they are! The trick is to focus on the two needles that you're currently using, and let the other needles hold your other stitches until you get around to them.

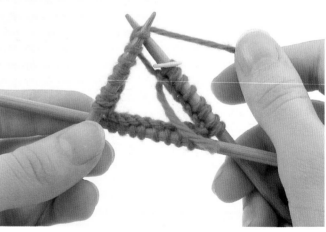

1 Begin by using just one needle to cast on all of your stitches. Then, distribute the stitches onto three needles. (If you're working with a large number of stitches, you can place your stitches onto four needles and knit with the fifth needle.) Hold the needle with the attached yarn in your right hand. To make sure that you aren't twisting the stitches, align the cast-on edge to the insides of the needles.

2 If you are using a stitch marker to keep track of the beginning of your rounds, slip the marker onto the needle in your right hand, and knit the first stitch from the left needle onto the right. (If you're beginning with a very small number of stitches, you can do this step at the beginning of a subsequent round, after you've increased your total number of stitches.)

3 Now use a fourth needle to knit the stitches on the needle in your left hand.

4 When you finish knitting from the needle in your left hand, the stitches will all end up on the right needle. Slide these stitches down a bit on the right needle so that they won't slip off. Then continue knitting the stitches on the next needle to the left onto your now-empty needle.

5 Sometimes, a column of loose stitches can form because of the gaps between the needles (often called the "ladder" effect.) To avoid this, you can keep your tension even by shifting the stitches around the needles every few rounds. Do this by setting aside the fourth needle and knitting two stitches directly from one needle to another.

6 Continue knitting from the needle in your left hand to the needle in your right, around and around, slipping the stitch marker along when you come to it. After knitting a few rounds, you will see a three-dimensional shape begin to form.

Starting Off with a Small Number of Stitches

Many of the patterns in this book begin with only six stitches on the needles, and then increase that number in the first round. If you're having trouble starting out with only two stitches per needle, you can begin by knitting the first round as you would an I-cord.

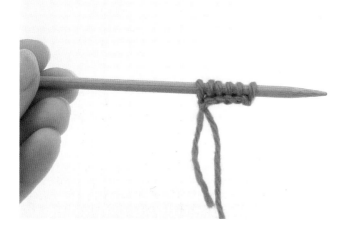

1 After casting on, leave your stitches on just one double-pointed needle and slide the end that doesn't have the yarn attached to the right side.

2 Bring the attached yarn around the back, and, pulling tightly on the yarn, knit onto a second needle. (In most patterns, you will work a kfb increase.)

3 Once you have finished knitting the stitches on the needle and have increased the total number of stitches, distribute the stitches onto three double-pointed needles and continue knitting in the round.

THE STUFFING

It's best to stuff your toy before the circumference of your knitting becomes too small. Err on the side of over-stuffing, but if you begin to see the stuffing showing between your stitches, either remove some stuffing or re-knit the piece on a smaller-size needle. (See Gauge on page 00.)

1 If you're using polyester stuffing, rip out a small handful of stuffing from the bag, and fluff it up by pulling it apart in your hands. Insert the stuffing into your toy, and add more fluffed-up stuffing as needed.

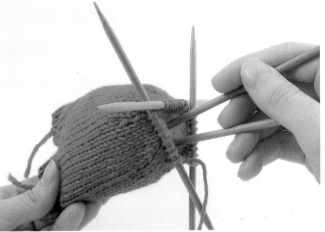

2 For stuffing thin appendages, use a knitting needle to gently nudge the stuffing into the smaller parts. I also find that holding two needles together like chopsticks works well for grabbing onto the stuffing from the inside and placing it exactly where I want it.

3 If you still have some small nooks and crannies to fill, you can also move the stuffing around from the outside with a knitting needle. (Just be sure not to stretch the yarn and create a big hole as you're doing so!)

4 When your toy is fully stuffed, finish the knitting. If you find that you need to add just a bit more stuffing at the top before closing up, using the two needles like chopsticks works well.

THE CLOSING

Most toy pieces end with instructions to "break yarn and draw tightly through sts with tapestry needle." Here's how.

1 When you are finished knitting and are ready to close up the piece, cut the yarn, leaving a 5-inch tail, and thread the end through a tapestry needle. Beginning with the first stitch in the round, thread the tapestry needle purlwise (from back to front) through each of the stitches in order in the round.

2 Pull the end of the cut yarn tightly to draw the stitches closed.

3 To secure, thread the loose end of yarn down through the hole that you just closed up and weave it through the toy.

THE EYES

Eyes will transform your toy into a sentient being that may or may not resent you. Here are my two favorite ways to give a toy the gift of vision.

Plastic Safety Eyes

Safety eyes come with a backing that snaps in place to hold the eyes securely. Despite their name, safety eyes can be pulled out between stitches, and so should not be used in toys for kids ages 3 and under.

You need to insert the backing on the wrong side of your knitting, so you'll attach these eyes before you close up your toy's body. If you have large hands, don't wait until you are about to draw your stitches closed; by then, the opening is pretty small. When attaching the eyes, the flatter side of the backing is placed up against the back of the black eyeball.

1 After you've stuffed the body, insert the front halves of the eyes where you would like them on the toy.

2 Reach inside the toy to snap the backs in place.

3 Once the eyes are attached, draw your stitches closed.

Once the eyes are snapped in place, they're meant to stay permanently in place. However, with the smaller sizes of plastic eyes (9mm and under), if you decide that you want to move the eyes after you've already attached the backs, you may be able to change their placement by popping the eye back inside the toy, then popping the eyeball out again in a different place. This only works if your knitting is relatively loose.

Another simple way to add eyes is to embroider them on with yarn and a tapestry needle. You can do this after the toy is finished and sewn up.

Locate where you would like to place the eye, and decide how big you would like your eye to be. For a medium-size eye, you will make a horizontal stitch that spans the width of 1½ knitted stitches.

1 Thread a piece of contrasting-color yarn onto the tapestry needle. Insert the needle in the back of the body, and bring it out where you want to begin the eye. Because this yarn will stay in place with the stitches you make, don't worry about securing it with a knot.

2 Insert the needle 1½ stitches, or three stitch legs, to the right, and bring it out again in the same place where you started.

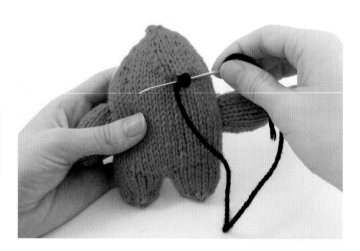

EYE SHAPES

To get a rounder eye, keep adding stitches, making the ones at the top and bottom of the eye slightly tighter than the ones in the middle section of the eye.

For a larger eye, start out making bigger stitches, spanning 2 or 2½ knitted stitches.

For a tiny eye, make just one stitch across ½ of a knitted stitch, or one strand of yarn.

3 Make 3 or 4 more stitches this way, with your needle going in and out of the same places.

THE SEAMING

Mattress Stitch

Now that you've knit up the pieces for your toy, it's time to put everything together. Meet your new friend: the mattress stitch.

Mattress stitch is a technique that allows you to stitch pieces together, working on the right side for an almost invisible seam. It's easy, but there are a few variations that are helpful to know, including some techniques that are specific to knitted toys.

The following steps show how to seam knitted pieces together on the knit side. You can also use mattress stitch to seam pieces that are purl side out and pieces with other stitch patterns. The trick is to make your stitches even and to keep the tension relatively tight, so that the pieces are drawn close together.

(Although you would normally use the same color yarn when seaming, a contrasting color is used here so that the stitches are more visible.)

Vertical Mattress Stitch

Use this variation when you are seaming two pieces together side by side, with two vertical rows of stitches lining up.

1 On one piece, locate the first stitch on the edge of the piece, and slip the tapestry needle under the horizontal bar that appears between this stitch and the next one in from the edge. Pull the yarn through.

2 Slip the needle under the corresponding bar on the second piece.

3 Go back to the first piece, and slip the needle under the next bar up. Go back and forth in this way a few times.

4 When you pull the yarn tight, the seam will disappear. Continue stitching the rest of the seam.

Horizontal Mattress Stitch

Use this variation when you are seaming cast-on or bound-off edges, with two horizontal rows of stitches lining up.

1 Slip the needle under the point of the V of the first stitch on the edge of one piece and pull the yarn through.

2 Slip your needle under the point of the corresponding V on the other piece.

3 Go back and forth in this way for several stitches.

4 Pull the yarn tightly and the seam will disappear.

Switching from Vertical to Horizontal Mattress Stitch

To switch from vertical mattress stitch to horizontal mattress stitch to turn a corner, simply change from one to the other when you reach the corner.

1 Once you finish the last stitch in your vertical seaming, having just inserted the needle under a bar on one piece, slip the needle under the first stitch's V on the other piece. Continue with horizontal mattress stitch.

2 Once you have made a few horizontal stitches, you may find it helpful to push in the corner a bit before pulling the yarn tightly to make the seam on the corner disappear.

Horizontal-to-Vertical Mattress Stitch

To seam two pieces whose stitches run in opposite directions, you will combine the vertical mattress stitch and horizontal mattress stitch.

1 Slip the needle under the bar on the vertical piece and under the V on the horizontal piece. Continue to go back and forth in this way for a few stitches.

2 Because knitted stitches are wider than they are tall, you will have more bars than Vs. Make up for this difference by slipping the needle under two bars instead of just one every few stitches.

Perpendicular Mattress Stitch

Most of the seaming that you'll do for toys will be with three-dimensional pieces instead of flat pieces. On these occasions, use perpendicular mattress stitch.

1 To attach an arm to a body, locate the place where you want to attach the arm and pin it in place.

2 Note that at the top and bottom, the stitches on the arm line up horizontally with the stitches on the body. Beginning at the top, use horizontal mattress stitch until the stitches no longer line up.

3 For the next stitch on the body, slip the needle diagonally down through the side of one knitted stitch and up through the middle of the stitch below it and to the left. Depending on the size of the appendage that you are attaching, you may need to make 1 or 2 more of these diagonal stitches on the body.

4 Now switch to vertical-to-horizontal mattress stitch, slipping the needle under the bars on the body and the Vs on the arm.

5 When the stitches stop lining up vertical to horizontal, again make one or more diagonal stitches on the body, then switch back to horizontal mattress stitch for the bottom of the arm. Continue to seam in a circle in this way until you come back to the place where you started. The result is an arm that sticks straight out from the body.

Angled Perpendicular Mattress Stitch

Sometimes you will want to attach arms and other limbs at an angle. Attach one arm straight out and one pointed down, and you have a toy that is either hailing a cab or giving a high five!

Begin seaming the same way as you would to attach the arm straight out, starting at the top of the arm, and making one or more diagonal stitches to follow the curve of the arm (Steps 2 and 3 of Perpendicular Mattress Stitch on page 30).

1 Now instead of slipping the needle under one bar on the body for every stitch V on the arm, slip it under two bars at a time for a few stitches in a row.

2 When you come to the armpit, use horizontal mattress stitch along the bottom of the arm, slipping the needle under stitches that are 3 or 4 stitches above the base of the arm piece. This will pull the arm down against the body.

3 When you finish seaming the bottom of the arm, make another diagonal stitch, then slip your needle under two bars at a time on the body, while stitching closer to the base of arm. Finish with perpendicular mattress stitch.

Backstitch

Backstitch is another seaming technique that you can use to attach a piece of flat knitting to a 3-dimensional piece. This simple stitching technique creates a secure seam.

1 Overlap the two pieces you want to attach. Insert the tapestry needle straight through both pieces, and bring it back out. Make the stitches the same length on top and underneath.

2 Insert the needle back down in the same place that you inserted it in Step 1, so that the second stitch abuts the first. Again, bring the needle back up at a distance equal to the length of one stitch.

3 Repeat Step 2 across the seam, then weave the loose end down through the pieces to secure it.

THE LOOSE ENDS

After knitting, stuffing, and seaming, your toy will probably have more than one loose end of yarn sticking out. How embarrassing!

1 To get rid of a loose end, thread it on a tapestry needle.

2 Insert the needle back through your toy and all the way out the other side. Just to be sure that the loose end won't work its way back out, you can weave in and out of the toy several times—just be careful that you don't pull it too tightly, or else you will end up with lumpy spots where the yarn is pulling on the fabric.

3 When your end is sufficiently woven in, cut the yarn short, pressing on the toy gently so that the end will be hidden inside the toy.

I'M SO EMBARRASSED!

THE EMBROIDERY

Sometimes eyes alone aren't enough, and you'll want to add other details. Using a tapestry needle and a contrasting color of yarn, you can give your toy a mouth, nose, hair, or a variety of personality-boosting features. I often use just one or two simple stitches. A little detail can go a long way.

Backstitch

In embroidery, backstitch is the best way to create a line on a single layer of your knitting, whether a curved or straight line. Lines can be mouths, eyebrows, or other details.

1 Start by making your first stitch, and bring your needle out where you want your second stitch to end.

2 Pull the yarn through, then insert the needle in the same place that you inserted it for the first stitch.

3 After repeating Steps 1 and 2 several times, you will have a line of stitches that lie right next to each other with no gaps between them. For a line that curves up or down, always remember to bring your needle out where you want your next stitch to end.

Duplicate Stitch

Duplicate stitch is a handy technique that gives the illusion of a change in color within the knitted fabric without having to actually work the new color into the knitting.

1 Bring your needle out from the middle of a stitch, just under the downward point of the stitch's V. Then insert your needle under the V immediately above.

2 Insert your needle back down in the same place you started to form one stitch. To make another duplicate stitch above this one, bring the needle back out immediately above the place where you inserted it.

3 The result is a stitch that "duplicates" the knitted stitch beneath it. Repeat Steps 1 and 2 for each stitch.

ADDITIONAL TECHNIQUES

Joining and Separating for Appendages

It's simple to make appendages like feet and ears as separate pieces to attach to a body, but sometimes it's better to integrate these parts into the knitting of the body for a seamless transition.

JOINING FEET AND OTHER APPENDAGES

In some patterns, two feet are knitted in the round separately, then joined together into one round to form a body. This technique can also be used to join together ears, arms, or other pairs that you want placed side by side.

Let's say you just finished making two feet. One foot will have the ball of yarn attached to it (Foot 1, in blue) and the other will have a loose tail of yarn (Foot 2, in pink). (The different colors are to help tell the two feet apart.)

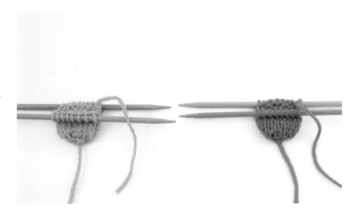

1 Divide the stitches of each foot onto 2 needles, with the same number of stitches on each needle. Place Foot 1 on the right, with the attached yarn on the right underside. Place Foot 2 on the left, with the cut yarn on the right underside.

2 With a fifth needle, knit the first half of stitches on Foot 1. If the pattern calls for it, cast on the specified number of stitches using a backward loop cast-on.

3 Leave the stitches on the second needle of Foot 1 unworked, and knit the stitches on both needles of Foot 2, beginning with the topmost needle. This will integrate Foot 2 into your round of knitting.

4 When you come to the loose end on Foot 2, wrap it around your working yarn to keep the stitches from loosening. You can later use this loose end to sew up the gap that will appear between the feet after you join them. Again, if the pattern calls for it, cast on the specified number of stitches using a backward loop cast-on.

5 Knit the remaining stitches from Foot 1.

6 Now all of your stitches are joined together into one round. Distribute the stitches onto 3 needles. Place marker, and you are ready to continue knitting in the round to form a body.

SEPARATING FOR EARS AND OTHER APPENDAGES

To make seamless ears at the top of your toy, you can use a technique that is basically the opposite of joining feet—separating one round of knitting into two separate rounds. You can use this technique to make legs or arms or any other pairs of appendages.

You will start with a round of stitches that you have worked—for ears, this will be the top of a body section that you just finished.

1 Divide the stitches onto four needles with the same number of stitches on each needle. For example, if you have 32 stitches in your row, place 8 stitches on each needle.

2 On the next round, knit the first needle of stitches. (The contrasting color yarn in the photos is for clarity.) Then, place the stitches from the next two needles onto a stitch holder to work later. There should be 16 stitches on the holder.

3 Knit the stitches on the last needle, pulling the yarn tightly across the space where the stitches are held. It helps to bunch up your held stitches onto one corner of the holder.

4 Divide your 16 working stitches onto 3 needles. Place marker, and work these stitches as indicated in the pattern.

5 When you have finished the first ear, break the yarn and draw the loose end through the stitches. For the second ear, place the stitches from the holder onto 3 needles, and attach the yarn to the last stitch—the stitch that comes before the gap—by weaving in the end with a tapestry needle.

6 Place marker and join in a round with the first stitch after the gap. Continue to work these stitches as indicated in the pattern to form the second ear. (Usually, there will be an extra round of knitting in the second ear because you won't use a round to divide the stitches as you did with the first ear.)

If there are no other openings in the piece, be sure to stuff before closing up the second ear.

CAN I HEAR YOU NOW?

Reattaching Yarn to Live Stitches

When you need to attach a new piece of yarn, you can usually tie it to the end of the piece you have been working with. In some cases, however, you need to reattach yarn without the help of another piece of yarn.

1 Thread the end of the yarn onto a tapestry needle, and slip the needle through a stitch next to the first stitch that you will knit with the new yarn. Bring the needle out on the back or purl side of the piece, then weave the loose end through a couple of stitches on the back of the piece.

2 Loop the end of the yarn through itself to secure it.

Picking up Stitches on a Three-Dimensional Piece

Another way to add appendages is to pick up stitches on the body of a toy and knit outward. This technique avoids seaming and it is ideal for small or thin appendages.

1 Turn the piece you are adding to (usually the toy's body) upside down, and decide where on the piece you want to pick up stitches. Beginning with the rightmost stitch, slip the tip of a double-pointed needle under the "bar" between knitted stitches on the body, and place the yarn between the tip of the needle and body, with the loose end on the right.

2 With the needle, pull the yarn from under the bar, creating a loop, as you would for a standard knit stitch.

3 For subsequent stitches, repeat Steps 1 and 2 with the bar immediately to the left on the body.

THE MAGIC LOOP

Knitting with a Circular Needle

All of the patterns in this book call for knitting with double-pointed needles, but if you prefer knitting with a circular needle, you can also knit small circumferences using the magic loop method. The length of the circular needle should be several times the length of your total number of stitches.

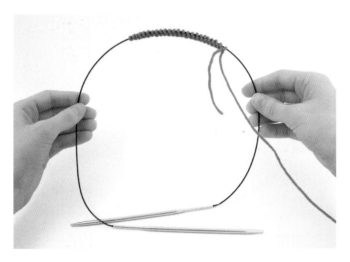

1 After casting on the designated number of stitches, slide all of the stitches down onto the flexible plastic cable.

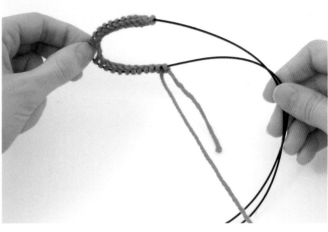

2 Divide the stitches into two groups, and fold the plastic in half between them, with the yarn attached to the group on the bottom. Grab onto the cable between the two groups of stitches.

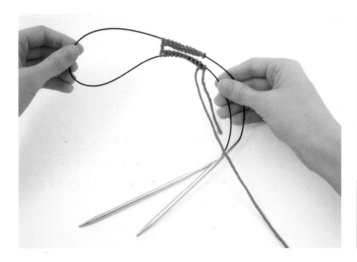

3 Pull on the cable between the stitches until you have a big loop pulled out.

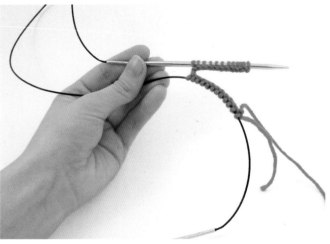

4 Slip the half of the stitches that doesn't have the yarn connected (the top group) down to one end of the needle. Keep the half with the yarn connected (the bottom group) on the cable, while still keeping the loop pulled out between the two groups.

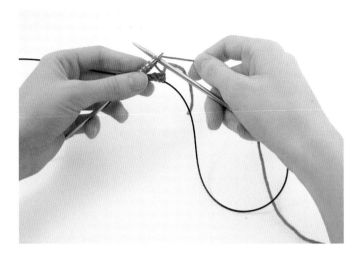

5 Make sure that the cast-on sides of your stitches are aligned, so that your knitting won't be twisted. Then, knit the stitches onto the empty end of the needle held in your right hand. You will have two loops of plastic cable on either side of your knitting.

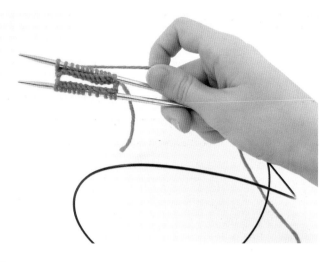

6 Once you finish knitting this half of the stitches, slide the other half of the stitches down to the other end of the needle, so that the two groups of stitches are on the two ends of the needle.

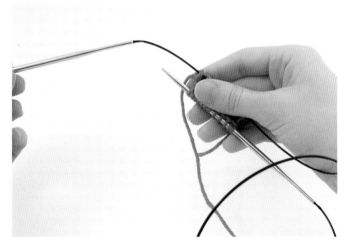

7 Slide the stiches you just finished knitting (with the yarn attached) down onto the cable.

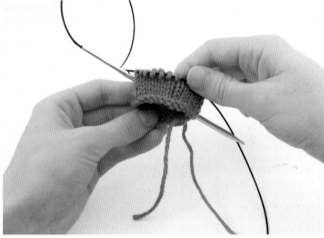

8 Flip the needle around so that the stitches are positioned as they were in Step 5, and knit the second set of stitches. Repeat Steps 5–8 to knit in the round. After a few rounds, you will see your circular piece take shape.

CHILDPROOFING
(AND ADULTPROOFING)
YOUR TOYS

Knitted toys look fabulous sitting on a shelf, but you can and should also play with them. Take a few precautions to make sure a toy will stand up to rough play by hands big and small.

Start with a tight gauge

The tighter your stitches are, the less likely that the toy will get pulled out of shape, the seams will come undone, or the plastic eyes will pop out. Of course, you don't want your stitches to be so tight that knitting is difficult or uncomfortable, so for most people, going down a needle size or two will be just right. (See "Gauge" on page 19 for more information.)

Secure pieces with extra stitches

Once you have finished attaching an arm, ear, or other appendage using mattress stitch or backstitch, you can make it more secure by going back and repeating all of the stitches in the seam. Just as in sewing projects, doubling up on your knitted seams will make the toy less likely to come apart.

Weave in loose ends more than once

Once you have attached an appendage as securely as possible, weave the loose end of your yarn in and out of your toy a few extra times so that it won't get pulled out accidentally. Just make sure that you don't pull the yarn too tightly—otherwise, you will create dimples in your toy from the yarn pulling on the knitted fabric.

KNITTING FOR SMALL CHILDREN

As with store-bought toys and clothes, extra precautions must be taken when knitting a toy for children ages 3 years and under.

No tiny toys

Very small toys, such as those featured in "Nano Knits," can be choking hazards. One safe way to use these patterns is to make them with thicker yarn and a larger gauge than the pattern calls for, so that you end up with a medium-size toy instead.

Skip the small pieces

If a toy has appendages smaller than $1^3/_4$ inches, it's best to leave out those parts altogether. For larger pieces, make sure to secure them and weave in loose ends securely as described above.

Embroider eyes and other details

Rather than attaching plastic eyes, buttons, or beads, use a contrasting-color yarn to embroider features onto your toy. Not only will it make the toy safer, but embroidery will give your toy its own unique look and personality.

CLEANING AND CARE

The choice of the yarn used determines how easy a toy is to clean, but even for toys made with superwash wool or other washable yarn, I recommend spot cleaning small stains to ensure the longest possible life for your toy. If your toy needs a thorough cleaning, wash by hand, reshape, and let it air dry completely before you store or play with it again.

Keep your toys out of direct sunlight when you're not playing with them because knitted fabric, like woven fabric, can fade with prolonged sun exposure. Also, keep your toys in a dry place so that they will live a long, happy life.

FIERCE
creatures

Aren't animals silly? They are
always getting into trouble, and most
of them are naked, too! Everyone
needs a knitted animal or ten.

Confused Moose

Bite-Free Bed Bugs

Pigs with Wigs

Squirrels on Wheels

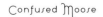

Baby Gators

CONFUSED MOOSE

This big guy thinks he's a bird! Just wait until he tries out those "wings."

TECHNIQUES » Kfb, k2tog, mattress stitch

YOU'LL NEED » Worsted-weight yarn in dark brown (MC), light brown (CC), three additional bird colors, orange, and black • Set of 7-inch size 6 US (4.0mm) double-pointed needles • Stitch holder • Safety eyes (size 9mm) • Tapestry needle • Stuffing • **Samples knit with** Cascade 220 (4/worsted weight; 100% wool; each approx 3½ oz/100g and 220 yds/201m) • 1 skein each 8686 (Brown) and 8622 (Camel) • <1 skein each 9478 (Cotton Candy), 7827 (Goldenrod), 8905 (Robin Egg Blue) • <1 skein each 9542 (Blaze) and 8555 (Black)

FINISHED SIZE » Moose approx 8 inches tall (including antlers); birds approx 1 inch tall

GAUGE » 2 inches = 10 stitches and 14 rows in stockinette stitch (knit on RS, purl on WS) on larger needles

> **MAKE ME FOR**
> Gentle giants

Note: The birds are not suitable for small children.

Feet

With CC and larger needles, CO 6 sts onto 3 needles and join in a rnd.

Rnd 1: [Kfb] 6 times (12 sts).

Rnd 2: [Kfb, k1] 6 times (18 sts).

Rnd 3: Knit

Switch to MC.

Rnd 4–6: Knit.

Break yarn, and place these 18 sts onto a holder.

Repeat Rnds 1–6 above to make another foot, without breaking yarn.

Join feet together

K9, and CO 3 sts using backward loop method. Place remaining 9 unworked sts onto one needle to work later.

Place 18 sts from holder onto two more needles, and with a fifth needle, k18. CO 3 sts using backward loop, then knit the remaining 9 sts from your other foot (42 sts). Distribute sts onto 3 needles, and place marker. You will continue to work in a rnd to form the body.

Body

Rnd 1 and all odd Rnds through Rnd 7: Knit.

Rnd 2: [Kfb, k5] 7 times (49 sts).

Rnd 4: [Kfb, k6] 7 times (56 sts).

Rnd 6: [Kfb, k7] 7 times (63 sts).

Rnd 8: [Kfb, k8] 7 times (70 sts).

Rnds 9 and 10: Knit.

Rnd 11: [Kfb, k9] 7 times (77 sts).

Rnds 12 and 13: Knit.

Rnd 14: [Kfb, k10] 7 times (84 sts).

Rnds 15–20: Knit 6 Rnds.

Rnd 21: [K10, k2tog] 7 times (77 sts).

Rnds 22 and 23: Knit.

Rnd 24: [K9, k2tog] 7 times (70 sts).

Rns 25 and 26: Knit.

Rnd 27: [K8, k2tog] 7 times (63 sts).

Rnds 28 and 29: Knit.

Rnd 30: [K7, k2tog] 7 times (56 sts).

Rnds 31 and 32: Knit.

Rnd 33: [K6, k2tog] 7 times (49 sts).

Rnds 34 and 35: Knit.

Rnd 36: [K5, k2tog] 7 times (42 sts).

Rnds 37 and 38: Knit.

Rnd 39: [K4, k2tog] 7 times (35 sts).

Rnds 40 and 41: Knit.

Rnd 42: [K3, k2tog] 7 times (28 sts).

Rnd 43: Knit.

Rnd 44: [K2, k2tog] 7 times (21 sts).

Rnd 45: Knit.

Stuff before continuing.

Rnd 46: [K1, k2tog] 7 times (14 sts).

Rnd 47: [K2tog] 7 times (7 sts).

Attach eyes, placed about 14 sts below top of body and 7 sts apart.

Break yarn and draw tightly through sts with tapestry needle.

Antlers (MAKE 2)

With CC and larger needles, CO 20 sts onto 3 needles, leaving a tail for seaming, and join in a rnd.

Rnds 1–12: Knit.

Rnd 13: [Kfb] twice, k2, place next 12 sts on a holder to work later, k2, [kfb] twice (12 sts).

Distribute 12 sts onto 3 needles to continue to work in a rnd.

Even Rnds 14–18: Knit.

Rnd 15: [Kfb] twice, k to last 2 sts, [kfb] twice (16 sts).

Rnd 17: Same as Rnd 15 (20 sts).

Rnd 19: Same as Rnd 15 (24 sts).

Rnds 20–22: Knit.

Rnd 23: [K2tog, k2] 6 times (18 sts).

Rnd 24: Knit.

Rnd 25: [K2tog, k1] 6 times (12 sts).

Rnd 26: [K2tog] 6 times (6 sts).

Break yarn and draw tightly through sts with tapestry needle.

Place 12 sts from holder onto 3 needles. Reattach yarn to last st, and join to work in a rnd.

Rnd 27: [Kfb] twice, k to last 2 sts, [kfb] twice (16 sts).

Rnd 28: Knit.

Rnd 29: Same as Rnd 27 (20 sts).

Rnds 30–33: Knit.

Rnds 34–47: Work same as Rnds 13–26, then break yarn and draw tightly through sts with tapestry needle.

Again, place 12 sts from holder onto 3 needles, reattach yarn to last st, and join to work in a rnd.

Rnds 48–50: Knit.

Rnd 51: [Kfb] twice, k to last 2 sts, [kfb] twice (16 sts).

Rnd 52: Knit.

Rnd 53: Same as Rnd 51 (20 sts).

Rnd 54: Knit.

Rnd 55: Same as Rnd 51 (24 sts).

Rnds 56–58: Knit.

Rnd 59: [K2tog, k2] 6 times (18 sts).

Rnd 60: Knit.

Rnd 61: [K2tog, k1] 6 times (12 sts).

Rnd 62: [K2tog] 6 times (6 sts).

Break yarn and draw tightly through sts with tapestry needle.

Arms (MAKE 2)

With MC and larger needles, CO 6 sts onto 3 needles, leaving a tail for seaming, and join in a rnd.

Rnd 1: [Kfb] 6 times (12 sts).

Rnd 2: [Kfb, k1] 6 times (18 sts).

Rnds 3–7: Knit.

Switch to CC.

Rnds 8 and 9: Knit.

Rnd 10: [K2tog, k1] 6 times (12 sts).

Stuff before continuing.

Rnd 11: [K2tog] 6 times (6 sts).

Break yarn and draw tightly through sts with tapestry needle.

Bird (MAKE LOTS!)

With smaller needles, CO 6 sts onto 3 needles and join in a rnd.

Rnd 1: [Kfb] 6 times (12 sts).

Rnd 2: Knit.

Rnd 3: [Kfb, k1] 6 times (18 sts).

Rnds 4–7: Knit 4 Rnds.

Rnd 8: [K2tog, k1] 6 times (12 sts).

Stuff before continuing.

Rnd 9: [K2tog] 6 times (6 sts).

Break yarn and draw tightly through sts with tapestry needle.

Embroider features on bird with 5 horizontal stitches of orange for beak and one stitch of black for each eye.

Finishing

Insert more stuffing between moose's feet if necessary, then sew using mattress stitch.

With black yarn, embroider on nostrils about 5 sts beneath eyes and 4 sts apart from each other.

Sew up gaps between antler prongs, and stuff antlers firmly. Attach CO edge to sides of head using mattress stitch, with the top side of antler placed about 11 sts from top of moose's head.

Attach arms at a downward angle using mattress stitch.

Tack birds to antlers with a few sts, or safety pins.

Weave in all loose ends.

BABY GATORS

They came from the sewer... and now they're coming for your pets! They will also accept chewy candies.

TECHNIQUES » Kfb, k2tog, bobble stitch (see Stitch Pattern), mattress stitch

YOU'LL NEED » Worsted-weight yarn in green (MC) and yellow (CC) • Set of 5-inch size 6 US (4.0mm) double-pointed needles • Safety eyes (size 9mm) • Tapestry needle • Stuffing • **Samples knit with** Cascade 220 (4/ worsted weight; 100% wool; each approx 3½ oz/100g and 220 yds/201m) • <1 skein each 7814 (Chartreuse), 2409 (Palm), 9461 (Lime Heather) • <1 skein of 7827 (Goldenrod)

FINISHED SIZE » Approx 4½ inches long

GAUGE » 2 inches = 10 stitches and 14 rows in stockinette stitch (knit on RS, purl on WS)

STITCH PATTERN » Bobble Stitch: Knit into front and back of stitch (kfb) twice before slipping stitch off left needle. Then, beginning with the rightmost stitch, pass the first, second, and third stitches on your right needle over the fourth (leftmost) stitch on your right needle.

Body

With MC, CO 6 sts onto 3 needles and join in a rnd.

Rnd 1: Knit.

Rnd 2 and all even Rnds (unless noted otherwise): Knit.

Rnd 3: P1, k1, p1, k3.

Rnds 5 and 7: Same as Rnd 3.

Rnd 8: [Kfb, k1] 3 times (9 sts). Place marker.

Rnd 9: [K1, p1] twice, k5.

Rnds 11 and 13: Same as Rnd 9.

Rnd 14: Kfb, k3, kfb, k1, kfb, k2 (12 sts).

Rnd 15: [K1, p2] twice, k6.

Rnds 17 and 19: Same as Rnd 15.

Rnd 20: Kfb, k5, [kfb, k2] twice (15 sts).

Rnd 21: K2, p2, k1, p2, k8.

Rnd 23: Same as Rnd 21.

Rnd 24: K9, kfb, k2, kfb, k1, kfb (18 sts).

Rnd 25: [K1, p3] twice, k10.

Rnds 27, 29, 31 and 33: Same as Rnd 25.

Separate top jaw

Begin the first rnd as usual, then switch to straight knitting in the first rnd.

Row 34: K1, kfb, k5, kfb, k1, and place remaining 9 sts on one needle to work later.

You should now have 11 sts on your needles. Place these 11 sts onto one needle to work straight, and turn.

Row 35: Purl.

Row 36: K3, bobble1, k3, bobble1, k3.

Row 37: Purl.

Row 38: K3, k2tog, k1, ssk, k3 (9 sts).

Rows 39–43: Beginning with a purl row, work 5 rows St st.

Row 44: K3, bobble1, k1, bobble1, k3.

Row 45: P1, p2tog, p3, p2tog, p1. (7 sts).

Row 46: K3tog, k1, k3tog (3 sts).

Switch to CC.

Row 47: Purl.

Row 48: [Kfb] 3 times (6 sts).

MAKE ME FOR
Urban legend lovers
or debunkers

A When you finish working the bottom jaw in rows, join the mouth lining and continue working in the round.

B Use yellow yarn and the mattress stitch to seam the mouth lining to the gator's jaws.

Row 49: Purl.

Row 50: K1, kfb, k2, kfb, k1 (8 sts).

Rows 51–55: Beginning with a purl row, work 5 rows St st.

Row 56: K1, kfb, k4, kfb, k1 (10 sts).

Rows 57: Purl.

Break yarn and place these 10 sts on one needle to work later.

Work bottom jaw

Reattach MC to your 9 held sts to work straight.

Row 58: K1, k2tog, k3, ssk, k1 (7 sts).

Rows 59–61: Work 3 rows St st.

Row 62: K1, k2tog, k1, ssk, k1 (5 sts).

Rows 63–67: Work 5 rows St st.

Row 68: K1, k3tog, k1 (3 sts).

Switch to CC.

Row 69: Purl.

Row 70: K1, kfb, k1 (4 sts).

Rows 71–73: Work 3 rows St st.

Row 74: K1, [kfb] twice, k1 (6 sts).

Rows 75–79: Work 5 rows St st, finishing with a purl row.

Row 80: Knit 6, then instead of turning, knit across 10 sts on other needle.

Distribute 16 sts onto 3 needles, and join to continue to work in a rnd. The resulting piece will look like a smaller, yellow alligator joined at the lips to your green gator (A, above).

Rnds 81–88: Knit 8 Rnds.

Rnd 89: [K2tog, k2] 4 times (12 sts).

Rnds 90–93: Knit 4 Rnds.

Rnd 94: [K2tog] 6 times (6 sts).

Break yarn and draw tightly through sts with tapestry needle.

Feet (MAKE 4)

With MC, CO 6 sts onto 1 needle to work as I-cord, leaving a tail for seaming.

Knit 3 Rnds.

Next rnd: [K2tog] 3 times (3 sts).

Knit 2 Rnds.

Next rnd: [Kfb] 3 times (6 sts).

Knit 1 more rnd, then break yarn and draw tightly through sts with tapestry needle.

Finishing

Weave in all loose ends except for the tails on the feet.

Attach safety eyes directly under the first two bobbles on the head.

Lightly stuff tail and fold yellow inner lining into body. Add a little more stuffing to the head, between the eyes.

Attach lining to top and bottom jaws using mattress stitch, beginning at the top front of jaw, sewing around to the bottom and continuing around the other side (B, above).

Attach feet to body at a forward-pointed angle.

BITE-FREE BED BUGS

Never sleep alone again with these innocuous cuddly bugs!

TECHNIQUES » Kfb, k2tog, mattress stitch

YOU'LL NEED » Worsted-weight yarn in three colors, plus small amount of black • Set of 5-inch size 6 US (4.0mm) double-pointed needles • Tapestry needle • Stuffing • Samples knit with Cascade 220 (4/worsted weight; 100% wool; each approx 3½ oz/100g and 220 yds/201m) • <1 skein 8905 (Robin Egg Blue), 9076 (Mint), 7809 (Violet), 8555 (Black) for bugs • <1 skein 9469 (Hot Pink), 8505 (White) for night cap

FINISHED SIZE » Approx 4 inches long

GAUGE » 2 inches = 10 stitches and 14 rows in stockinette stitch (knit on RS, purl on WS)

Body

CO 6 sts onto 3 needles and join in a rnd.

Rnd 1: [Kfb] 6 times (12 sts). Place marker.

Rnd 2: [Kfb, k1] 6 times (18 sts).

Rnd 3: Knit.

Rnd 4: [Kfb, k2] 6 times (24 sts).

Rnd 5: Knit.

Rnd 6: [Kfb, k3] 6 times (30 sts).

Rnds 7 and 8: Knit.

Rnd 9: [Kfb, k4] 6 times (36 sts).

Rnds 10–12: Knit.

Rnd 13: [K4, k2tog] 6 times (30 sts).

Rnds 14 and 15: Knit.

Rnd 16: [K3, k2tog] 6 times (24 sts).

Rnd 17: Knit.

Rnd 18: [K2, k2tog] 6 times (18 sts).

Rnd 19: [K1, k2tog] 6 times (12 sts).

MAKE US FOR
Late sleepers who love surprises

Rnd 20: [kfb, k1] 6 times (18 sts).

Rnd 21: Knit.

Rnd 22: [Kfb, k2] 6 times (24 sts).

Rnds 23 and 24: Knit.

Rnd 25: [Kfb, k3] 6 times (30 sts).

Rnds 26 and 27: Knit.

Rnd 28: [K3, k2tog] 6 times (24 sts).

Rnds 29 and 30: Knit.

Rnd 31: [K2, k2tog] 6 times (18 sts).

Rnd 32: Knit.

Stuff piece before continuing.

Rnd 33: [K1, k2tog] (12 sts).

Rnd 34: [K2tog] 6 times (6 sts).

Add a little more stuffing to top, then break yarn and draw tightly through stitches with tapestry needle.

Antennae (MAKE 2)

CO 6 sts onto 3 needles, leaving a tail for seaming, and join in a rnd.

Knit 3 Rnds, then break yarn and draw tightly through stitches with tapestry needle.

Feet (MAKE 6)

CO 8 sts onto 3 needles, leaving a tail for seaming, and join in a rnd.

Knit 4 Rnds, then break yarn and draw tightly through stitches with tapestry needle.

Finishing

For each eye, use black yarn and tapestry needle to embroider a large V shape with 2 stitches.

Lightly stuff antennae, and attach to head using mattress stitch. Lightly stuff feet, line up 3 feet along each side of body and attach using mattress stitch.

Weave in all loose ends.

Night Cap

With main color yarn, CO 24 sts onto 3 needles, place marker, and join in a rnd.

Rnds 1–4: Knit.

Rnd 5: [K2tog, k4] 4 times (20 sts).

Rnds 6 and 7: Knit.

Rnd 8: [K2og, k3] 4 times (16 sts).

Rnds 9–14: Knit 6 Rnds.

Rnd 15: [K2tog, k2] 4 times (12 sts).

Rnds 16–19: Knit 4 Rnds.

Rnd 20: [K2tog, k1] 4 times (8 sts).

Rnds 21–24: Knit 4 Rnds.

Break yarn and draw tightly through sts.

With a contrasting color yarn and tapestry needle, embroider stars on cap, with 3 crossed stitches per star. Fold down top half of hat and tack in place. Weave in loose ends.

PIGS WITH WIGS

This is what happens when you let the pigs get into the piggy bank. Such extravagance is appalling!

Awesome Afro   Magnificent Mohawk

TECHNIQUES » Kfb, k2tog, k3tog, I-cord, picking up stitches, mattress stitch

YOU'LL NEED » Worsted-weight yarn in pink, 4 wig colors, white, and small amount of black • Set of 6-inch size 6 US (4.0mm) double-pointed needles • Stitch marker • Safety eyes (size 9mm) • Tapestry needle • Stuffing • Samples knit with Cascade 220 (4/worsted weight; 100% wool; each approx 3½ oz/100g and 220 yds/201m • 1 skein 9478 (Cotton Candy); <1 skein each 7808 (Purple Hyacinth), 9421 (Blue Hawaii), 7827 (Goldenrod), 7814 (Chartreuse), 8505 (White) • <1 yard 8555 (Black)

FINISHED SIZE » Approx 6½ inches long

GAUGE » 2 inches = 10 stitches and 14 rows in stockinette stitch (knit on RS, purl on WS)

Body

CO 6 sts onto 3 needles and join in a rnd.

Rnd 1: [Kfb] 6 times (12 sts). Place maker.

Rnd 2: [Kfb, k1] 6 times (18 sts).

Odd Rnds 3–15: Knit.

Rnd 4: [Kfb, k2] 6 times (24 sts).

Rnd 6: [Kfb, k3] 6 times (30 sts).

Rnd 8: [Kfb, k4] 6 times (36 sts).

Rnd 10: [Kfb, k5] 6 times (42 sts).

Rnd 12: [Kfb k6] 6 times (48 sts).

Rnd 14: [Kfb, k7] 6 times (54 sts).

Rnd 16: [Kfb, k8] 6 times (60 sts).

Rnds 17–36: Knit 20 Rnds.

Rnd 37: [K2tog, k8] 6 times (54 sts).

Even Rnds 38–46: Knit.

Rnd 39: [K2tog, k7] 6 times (48 sts).

Rnd 41: [K2tog, k6] 6 times (42 sts).

Rnd 43: [K2tog, k5] 6 times (36 sts).

Rnd 45: [K2tog, k4] 6 times (30 sts).

Rnd 47: [K2tog, k3] 6 times (24 sts).

Rnds 48–51: Knit 4 Rnds.

Stuff before continuing.

Rnd 52: [K2tog, k1] 8 times (16 sts).

Rnd 53: Knit.

Rnd 54: [K2tog] 8 times (8 sts).

Attach eyes along two decrease seams (with one seam in between), placed about 6 sts back from the point at which you began knitting straight for snout (Rnd 48).

Add a bit more stuffing into snout, then break yarn and draw tightly through sts with tapestry needle.

Beautiful Beehive

MAKE US FOR
Your favorite stylist or wig-maker (doesn't everyone have one?)

Ears (MAKE 2)

CO 10 sts onto one needle to work straight, leaving a tail for seaming.

Row 1: Purl.

Row 2: K1, k2tog, k4, k2tog, k1 (8 sts).

Rows 3–7: Work 5 rows St st.

Row 8: K1, [k2tog] 3 times, k1 (5 sts).

Row 9: Purl.

Row 10: K1, k3tog, k1 (3 sts).

Break yarn and draw tightly through sts with tapestry needle.

Feet (MAKE 4)

CO 12 sts onto 3 needles, leaving a tail for seaming, and join in a rnd.

Knit 6 Rnds.

Next rnd: [K2tog] 6 times (6 sts).

Break yarn and draw tightly through sts with tapestry needle.

Tail

CO 30 sts onto one needle to work straight.

K2tog, [k2tog, pass rightmost stitch over] repeat to end, binding off as you go until the last st is bound off.

TIP: To make your tail as curly as possible, cast on loosely, then use a tighter tension when binding off.

Finishing

Thread loose end attached to pig's nose down through the middle of the sts that you closed up, and shape to make a flat nose.

Stuff feet, and attach to underside of pig using mattress stitch.

Sew ears to head using mattress stitch, sewing the CO edge on in a curved shape.

Tack tail to pig's behind, with the tail pointed upward.

With black yarn and tapestry needle, embroider two long vertical stitches onto flat part of nose.

Weave in all loose ends.

Beautiful Beehive Wig

(WORKED FROM BOTTOM TO TOP)

CO 4 sts onto one needle.

Rnd 1 (work as I-cord): [Kfb] 4 times (8 sts).

Distribute sts onto 3 needles, place marker, and join in a rnd.

Rnd 2: [Kfb] 8 times (16 sts).

Odd Rnds 3–9: Knit.

Rnd 4: [Kfb, k1] 8 times (24 sts).

Rnd 6: [Kfb, k2] 8 times (32 sts).

Rnd 8: [Kfb, k3] 8 times (40 sts).

Rnd 10: [Kfb, k4] 8 times (48 sts).

Rnds 11–18: [K3, p1, k3, p1] 6 times (8 Rnds).

Rnd 19: [K2tog, k1, p1, k3, p1] 6 times (42 sts).

Rnd 20: [K2, p1, k3, p1] 6 times.

Rnd 21: [K2tog, p1, k3, p1] 6 times (36 sts)

Rnd 22: [K1, p1, k3, p1] 6 times.

Rnd 23: [K2tog, k3, p1] 6 times (30 sts).

Rnd 24: [Kfb, k3, p1] 6 times (36 sts).

Rnd 25: [K5, p1] 6 times.

Rnd 26: [Kfb, p1, k3, p1] 6 times (42 sts).

Rnds 27–30: [K2, p1, k3, p1] 6 times (4 Rnds).

Rnd 31: [K2tog, p1, k3, p1] 6 times (36 sts).

Rnd 32: [K1, p1, k3, p1] 6 times.

Rnd 33: [K2tog, k3, p1] (30 sts).

Rnd 34: [K4, p1] 6 times.

Rnd 35: [K2tog, k2, p1] 6 times (24 sts).

Rnd 36: [Kfb, k2, p1] 6 times (30 sts).

Rnd 37: [K4, p1] 6 times.

Rnd 38: [Kfb, k3, p1] 6 times (36 sts).

Rnds 39 and 40: [K2, p1] 12 times.

Rnd 41: [K2tog, p1, k2, p1] 6 times (30 sts).

Rnd 42: [K1, p1, k2, p1] 6 times.

Rnd 43: [K2tog, k2, p1] 6 times (24 sts).

Rnd 44: [K3, p1] 6 times.

Rnd 45: [K2tog, k1, p1] 6 times (18 sts).

Rnd 46: [K2, p1] 6 times.

Stuff before continuing.

Rnd 47: [K2tog, p1] 6 times (12 sts).

Rnd 48: [K2tog] 6 times (6 sts).

Break yarn and draw tightly through sts with tapestry needle.

Beehive Curls (MAKE 6)

Work same as pig's tail, but with same color yarn as Beehive.

Finishing Beehive

Tack three curls on each side of beehive. If necessary, massage piece into curvy beehive shape.

Weave in loose ends.

Beehive Strap

With white yarn, pick up and knit 3 sts on underside of piece, close to the edge.

Knit I-cord until approx 8½ inches long, and BO.

Repeat for second strap on opposite side of underside of piece.

Weave in all loose ends.

Awesome Afro Wig

(WORKED FROM BOTTOM TO TOP)

CO 4 sts onto one needle.

Rnds 1–10: Work same as Beehive pattern (48 sts).

Rnd 11: Kfb, [k1, p1] to end (49 sts).

Rnd 12: [P1, k1] to end.

Rnd 13: [K1, p1] to end.

Rnd 14: P1, [kfb] twice, [k1, p1] 5 times, [kfb] twice, [k1, p1] 5 times, [kfb] twice, [k1, p1] 5 times, [kfb] twice, [k1, p1] 5 times (57 sts).

Rnds 15–17: Work as est.

Rnd 18: P1, [kfb] twice, [k1, p1] 6 times, [kfb] twice, [k1, p1] 6 times, [kfb] twice, [k1, p1] 6 times, [kfb] twice, [k1, p1] 6 times (65 sts).

Rnds 19–21: Work as est.

Rnd 22: P1, [k1, p1] 6 times, k2tog, p2tog, [k1, p1] 6 times, k2tog, p2tog, [k1, p1] 6 times, k2tog, p2tog, [k1, p1] 6 times, k2tog, p2tog (57 sts).

Rnds 23–25: Work as est.

Rnd 26: P1, [k1, p1] 5 times, k2tog, p2tog, [k1, p1] 5 times, k2tog, p2tog, [k1, p1] 5 times, k2tog, p2tog, [k1, p1] 5 times, k2tog, p2tog (49 sts).

Rnds 27–29: Work as est.

Rnd 30: P1, [k1, p1] 4 times, k2tog, p2tog, [k1, p1] 4 times, k2tog, p2tog, [k1, p1] 4 times, k2tog, p2tog, [k1, p1] 4 times, k2tog, p2tog (41 sts).

Rnds 31 and 32: Work as est.

Rnd 33: K1, [p1, k1] 3 times, p2tog, k2tog, [p1, k1] 3 times, p2tog, k2tog, [p1, k1] 3 times, p2tog, k2tog, [p1, k1] 3 times, p2tog, k2tog (33 sts).

Rnds 34 and 35: Knit.

Rnd 36: P1, [k1, p1] twice, k2tog, p2tog, [k1, p1] twice, k2tog, p2tog, [k1, p1] twice, k2tog, p2tog, [k1, p1] twice, k2tog, p2tog (25 sts).

Rnd 37: Work as est.

Rnd 38: P1, k1, p1, k2tog, p2tog, k1, p1, k2tog, p2tog, k1, p1, k2tog, p2tog, k1, p1, k2tog, p2tog (17 sts).

Stuff piece before continuing.

Rnd 39: K3tog, [p2tog, k2tog] 3 times, p2tog (8 sts).

Break yarn and draw tightly through sts with tapestry needle.

Sideburns for Afro (MAKE 2)

CO 8 sts onto one needle to work straight.

Rows 1 and 2: Knit.

Row 3: K1, k2tog, k2, k2tog, k1 (6 sts).

Rows 4–6: Knit.

Row 7: K1, [k2tog] twice, k1 (4 sts).

Rows 8–15: Knit 8 rows.

BO all sts.

Finishing Afro

Attach BO edges of sideburns to sides of Afro using tapestry needle and backstitch.

Weave in all loose ends.

Straps for Afro

Work same as Straps for Beehive.

Buxom Bob Wig

CO 30 sts onto 3 needles, leaving a long tail for seaming. Place maker and join in a rnd.

Rnds 1–4: Knit.

Rnd 5: Kfb, k12, [k2tog] twice, k12, kfb.

Rnds 6 and 7: Knit.

Rnd 8: Work same as Rnd 5.

Rnds 9 and 10: Knit.

Rnd 11: Work same as Rnd 5.

Rnds 12–51: Knit 40 Rnds.

Rnd 52: K2tog, k12, [kfb] twice, k12, k2tog.

Rnds 53 and 54: Knit.

Rnd 55: Work same as Rnd 52.

Rnds 56 and 57: Knit.

Rnd 58: Work as as Rnd 52.

Rnds 59 and 60: Knit.

BO all sts, and leave a long tail for seaming.

Buxom Bob

Bangs for Bob

CO 10 sts onto one needle to work straight.

Row 1: Purl.

Row 2: K1, kfb, k to last 2 sts, kfb, k1 (12 sts).

Rows 3–5: Beginning with a purl row, work in St st.

Row 6: K1, kfb, k to last 2 sts, kfb, k1 (14 sts.)

Rows 7–9: Beginning with a purl row, work in St st.

Row 10: K1, k2tog, k to last 3 sts, k2tog, k1 (12 sts).

Rows 11–13: Work in St st.

Row 14: K1, k2tog, k to last 3 sts, k2tog, k1 (10 sts).

Row 15: Purl.

BO all sts.

Finishing Bob

Lay wig flat, so that it lies in a crescent shape. Lightly stuff, and sew up the two open ends using mattress stitch.

Locate the place where the middle "part" should go, and with same color yarn as Bob, sew a line of backstitch going straight through both layers of wig, with one stitch per knitted stitch. Make sure that you keep an equal amount of stuffing on the left and right sides of wig.

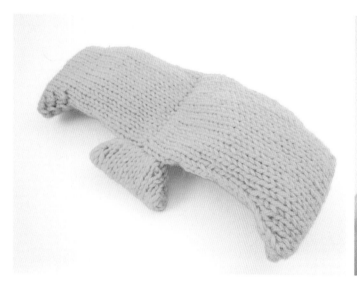

A After lightly stuffing and seaming, your finished Bob wig should lie flat with a "part" in the middle.

B Fold the Spikes in half and align needle with held stitches to rejoin.

Fold bangs in half so that the CO edge meets the BO edge, and sew around the open sides using mattress stitch. Attach the narrower CO/BO edge of bangs to front-middle of Bob, again using mattress stitch to sew on the top and bottom sides (A, above).

Weave in all loose ends.

Straps for Bob

With white yarn, pick up and knit 3 sts on underside of Bob, about 5 sts from the side seam and 6 sts from the front.

Knit I-cord until approx 6½ inches long, and BO. Repeat for opposite strap, and weave in all loose ends.

Magnificent Mohawk Wig

NOTE: You will flip this wig inside out after knitting.

CO 26 sts onto 3 needles, leaving a long tail for seaming. Place marker

and join in a rnd.

Rnd 1: Knit.

Rnd 2: Kfb, k11, [kfb] twice, k11, kfb (30 sts).

Rnd 3: Knit.

Rnd 4: Kfb, k13, [kfb] twice, k13, kfb (34 sts).

Rnds 5–14: Knit 10 Rnds.

Remove marker, and place first 17 sts in the rnd onto one needle and the last 17 onto another. You will continue to work the first 17 sts straight, leaving the last 17 on the other needle to join later.

Rows 15–53: Work as indicated in "Mohawk Spikes" chart.

Fold in half the long Spikes piece you just worked, so that the two needles—the one whose stitches you just worked and the one with the 17 held stitches—meet (B, above).

Distribute 34 sts onto 3 needles, and knit across the 17 held sts with a fourth needle.

Place marker, and rejoin to work in a rnd.

Rnds 54–63: Knit 10 Rnds.

Rnd 64: K2tog, k13, [k2tog] twice, k13, k2tog (30 sts).

Rnd 65: Knit.

Rnd 66: K2tog, k11, [k2tog] twice, k11, k2tog (26 sts).

Rnd 67: Knit.

BO all sts.

Finishing Mohawk

Turn piece inside out, so that the areas of purl sts face outside, and stripes of knit sts appear in the Spikes section.

The Spikes section will become the vertical part of the Mohawk. Keeping that section in the top middle, lay piece flat and seam up the open CO and BO edges of piece using tapestry needle and backstitch (C, above right).

Fold the Spikes section in half, so that it is perpendicular to the rest of

C Use a tapestry needle and mattress stitch to seam the two open ends of the Spikes.

the piece. Sew up one side using mattress stitch, slipping tapestry needle under two purl stitch "bumps" for each stitch. Stuff Spikes, and sew up opposite side.

Attach middle section to the base of the piece with a few more sts.

Straps for Mohawk

With white yarn, pick up and knit 3 sts on the side seam, about 5 sts in from the front.

Knit I-cord until approx 9 inches long, and BO.

Repeat for opposite strap.

Weave in all loose ends.

MOHAWK SPIKES

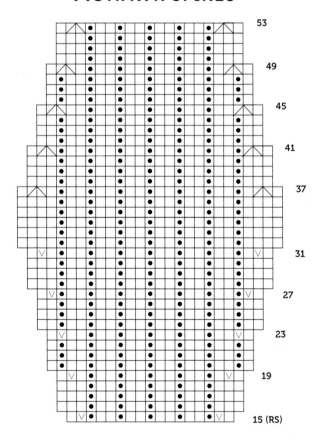

	Knit on RS, purl on WS
●	Purl on RS, knit on WS
∨	kfb
⋌⋋	k2tog

SQUIRRELS ON WHEELS

Every night is disco night for these rapid rodents.

TECHNIQUES » Kfb, k2tog, mattress stitch

YOU'LL NEED » Worsted-weight yarn in a main color (MC), contrasting color (CC), and a small amount of accent color • Set of 6-inch size 6 US (4.0mm) double-pointed needles • Safety eyes (size 9mm) • Tapestry needle • Stuffing • **Samples knit with** Cascade 220 (4/worsted weight; 100% wool; each approx 3½ oz/100g

and 220 yds/201m) • 1 skein 7821 (Sienna), <1 skein 8509 (Grey), and <1 yard 8555 (Black) for brown squirrel • 1 skein 7827 (Goldenrod), <1 skein 9444 (Tangerine Heather), and <1 yard 8686 (Brown) for yellow squirrel

FINISHED SIZE » Approx 5½ inches long

GAUGE » 2 inches = 10 stitches and 14 rows in stockinette stitch (knit on RS, purl on WS)

Body
(WORKED FROM TAIL TO NOSE)

With MC, CO 6 sts onto 3 needles and join in a rnd.

Rnd 1: Knit.

Rnd 2: [Kfb] 6 times (12 sts). Place marker.

Rnd 3: Knit.

Rnd 4: [Kfb, k1] 6 times (18 sts).

Rnds 5 and 6: Knit.

Rnd 7: [Kfb, k2] 6 times (24 sts).

Rnds 8 and 9: Knit.

Rnd 10: [Kfb, k3] 6 times (30 sts).

Rnds 11 and 12: Knit.

Rnd 13: [Kfb, k4] 6 times (36 sts).

Rnds 14 and 15: Knit.

Rnd 16: [Kfb, k5] 6 times (42 sts).

Rnds 17 and 18: Knit.

Rnd 19: [Kfb, k6] 6 times (48 sts).

Rnds 20–31: Knit 12 Rnds.

Rnd 32: [K2tog, k6] 6 times (42 sts).

Rnds 33–36: Knit 4 Rnds.

Rnd 37: [K2tog, k5] 6 times (36 sts).

Rnds 38–41: Knit 4 Rnds.

Rnd 42: [K2tog, k4] 6 times (30 sts).

Rnd 43: Knit.

Rnd 44: [K2tog, k3] 6 times (24 sts).

Rnd 45: Knit.

Rnd 46: [K2tog, k2] 6 times (18 sts).

Rnds 47 and 48: Knit.

Rnd 49: K1, kfb, k3, kfb, k2, [kfb twice, k2, kfb, k3, kfb, k1 (24 sts).

Rnd 50: Knit.

Rnd 51: K2, kfb, k3, kfb, k4, [kfb] twice, k4, kfb, k3, kfb, k2 (30 sts).

Rnds 52 and 53: Knit.

Rnd 54: K3, kfb, k3, kfb, k6, [kfb] twice, k6, kfb, k3, kfb, k3 (36 sts).

Rnds 55 and 56: Knit.

Rnd 57: K4, kfb, k3, kfb, k8, [kfb] twice, k8, kfb, k3, kfb, k4 (42 sts).

Rnds 58–61: Knit 4 Rnds.

Rnd 62: K5, kfb, k3, kfb, k10, [kfb] twice, k10, kfb, k3, kfb, k5 (48 sts).

MAKE US FOR
Speeders and squirrel-feeders

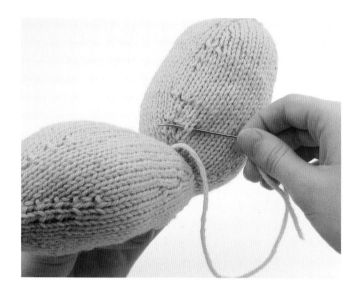

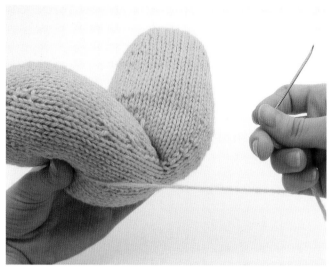

A Fold tail up and use the mattress stitch to attach it to the body, stitching across the fourth increase round on the body.

B When attaching the tail to the body, bring the tapestry needle all the way out through the back of the tail before inserting it again for the next stitch to the left.

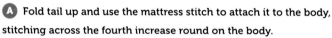

Rnds 63–72: Knit 10 Rnds.

Rnd 73: K5, k2tog, k3, k2tog, k10, [k2tog] twice, k10, k2tog, k3, k2tog, k5 (42 sts).

Rnds 74–77: Knit 4 Rnds.

Rnd 78: K4, k2tog, k3, k2tog, k8, [k2tog] twice, k8, k2tog, k3, k2tog, k4 (36 sts).

Rnds 79 and 80: Knit.

Rnd 81: K3, k2tog, k3, k2tog, k6, [k2tog] twice, k6, k2tog, k3, k2tog, k3 (30 sts).

Rnds 82 and 83: Knit.

Rnd 84: K2, k2tog, k3, k2tog, k4, [k2tog] twice, k4, k2tog, k3, k2tog, k2 (24 sts).

Rnd 85: Knit.

Stuff piece before continuing, making sure to fully stuff the tail section without over-stuffing.

Rnd 86: K1, k2tog, k3, k2tog, k2, [k2tog] twice, k2, k2tog, k3, k2tog, k1 (18 sts).

Rnd 87: Knit.

Rnd 88: K2tog, k3, [k2tog] 4 times, k3, k2tog (12 sts).

Rnd 89: [K2tog] 6 times (6 sts).

Locate the top of squirrel's head (opposite of the place where your Rnds began, which will be the middle bottom of the body), and attach eyes about 10 sts from front of body and spaced about 10 sts apart.

Add more stuffing to piece, then break yarn and draw tightly through sts with tapestry needle.

Ears (MAKE 2)

With MC, CO 10 sts onto 3 needles, leaving a tail for seaming, and join in a rnd.

Knit 5 Rnds.

Break yarn and draw tightly through sts with tapestry needle.

Wheels (MAKE 4)

With CC, CO 8 sts onto 3 needles and join in a rnd.

Rnd 1: Knit.

Rnd 2: [Kfb] 8 times (16 sts).

Rnd 3: Knit.

Rnd 4: [Kfb, k1] 8 times (24 sts).

Rnds 5–7: Knit.

Rnd 8: [K2tog, k1] 8 times (16 sts).

Rnd 9: Knit.

Rnd 10: [K2tog] 8 times (8 sts).

Rnd 11: Knit.

Stuff, then break yarn and draw tightly through sts with tapestry needle.

Finishing

Fold tail up against body at a

C Insert the tapestry needle back into the tail just above where you pulled it out, so that your stitches on the tail line up with your knitted stitches and are invisible.

D After attaching the tail to the body, you will have a nearly invisible seam going across the back of the tail.

90-degree angle (A, opposite, far left). Locate the point at which the tail meets up with the fourth increase rnd on the body section—this is where you will attach the tail to the body.

Beginning on the right side of the tail, attach tail to body using mattress stitch, with your stitches going all the way out the backside of the tail (B, opposite, near left).

When you insert your needle back into the tail, make a stitch that is aligned vertically with the knitted sts, so that it is invisible (C, above left). Make your stitches secure, but not too tight, so that the tail has a bit of a bend to it, but still has volume. Use about 8 stitches in total, or as many stitches as you need to secure the tail in place.

The seam will be nearly invisible on the back of the tail (D, above right).

Attach ears to body about 5 sts back from eyes using mattress stitch.

With accent color and tapestry needle, embroider an asterisk-shaped design at the closed off end of each wheel. Align wheels in four corners of body, and attach with mattress stitch. When tipped backward, the squirrel

should balance with its front wheels up in the air.

With accent colors, embroider on nose using four horizontal stitches across the closed up sts at front of body.

Weave in all loose ends.

RANDOM
objects

Shh, the toys in this section don't like the term "random junk." They prefer "categorically challenged."

Orbiting Oddity   »   Grouchy Couch   »   Cuter Polluters   »   Shyscrapers

TV Guy

ORBITING ODDITY

They come in peace, but they're more interested in this new "ragtime" music they've been picking up in outer space.

TECHNIQUES » Kfb, k2tog, stranded color knitting

YOU'LL NEED » Worsted-weight yarn in 4 colors: blue (Color 1), light blue (Color 2), black (Color 3), and small amount of yellow • Set of 7-inch size 5 US (3.75mm) double-pointed needles • Safety eyes (size 12mm) • Tapestry needle • Stuffing • Samples knit with Cascade 220 (4/worsted weight; 100% wool; each approx 3½ oz/100g and 220 yds/201m) • 1 skein of 8891 (Cyan Blue) • <1 skein each 9076 (Mint) and 8555 (Black) • <1 yard 7827 (Goldenrod)

FINISHED SIZE » Approx 3½ inches tall and 5 inches wide

GAUGE » 2 inches = 11 stitches and 15½ rows in stockinette stitch (knit on RS, purl on WS)

With Color 1, CO 4 sts onto one needle.

Rnd 1: (Work as I-cord): [Kfb] 4 times (8 sts).

Distribute sts onto 3 needles, place marker, and join in a rnd.

Rnd 2: [Kfb] 8 times (16 sts).

Odd rnds 3–29: Knit.

Rnd 4: [Kfb, k1] 8 times (24 sts).

Rnd 6: [Kfb, k2] 8 times (32 sts).

Rnd 8: [Kfb, k3] 8 times (40 sts).

Rnd 10: [Kfb, k4] 8 times (48 sts).

Rnd 12: [Kfb, k5] 8 times (56 sts).

Rnd 14: [Kfb, k6] 8 times (64 sts).

Rnd 16: [Kfb, k7] 8 times (72 sts).

Rnd 18: [Kfb, k8] 8 times (80 sts).

Rnd 20: [Kfb, k9] 8 times (88 sts).

Rnd 22: [Kfb, k10] 8 times (96 sts).

Rnd 24: Knit.

Rnd 26: [K2tog, k10] 8 times (88 sts).

Rnd 28: [K2tog, k9] 8 times (80 sts).

Rnd 30: [K2tog, k8] 8 times (72 sts).

Rnd 32: [K2tog, k7] 8 time (64 sts).

Rnd 34: [K2tog, k6] 8 times (56 sts).

Break yarn, and switch to Color 2.

Rnds 35–41: Refer to color chart, incorporating Color 3 with Color 2 as indicated.

Switch back to Color 1.

Rnd 42: [K2tog, k6] 7 times (49 sts).

Odd rnds 43–51: Knit.

Rnd 44: [K2tog, k5] 7 times (42 sts)

Rnd 46: [K2tog, k4] 7 times (35 sts).

Rnd 48: [K2tog, k3] 7 times (28 sts).

Rnd 50: [K2tog, k2] 7 times (21 sts).

Stuff before continuing, making sure to completely fill out the saucer part of the piece while keeping the bottom flat.

Attach eyes to saucer about 5 sts up from widest point and spaced 10 sts apart from each other.

Rnd 52: [K2tog, k1] 7 times (14 sts).

Rnd 53: [K2tog] to end (7 sts).

Add more stuffing to top of the piece, then break yarn and draw tightly through sts with tapestry needle.

Finishing

With yellow yarn and tapestry needle, embroider on aliens' eyes using one stitch per eye.

Weave in loose ends.

ALIEN COLOR PATTERN

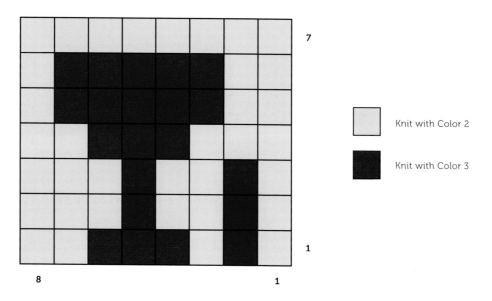

7

1

8   1

Repeat every 8 sts in rnd

Knit with Color 2

Knit with Color 3

GROUCHY COUCH

This fusty furnishing may have seen better decades, but then again, maybe so have you!

TECHNIQUES » Provisional cast-on, stranded color knitting, backward loop cast-on, mattress stitch, simple embroidery

YOU'LL NEED » Worsted-weight yarn in green (MC), orange (CC), and small amount of black • Set of 7-inch size 5 US (3.75mm) double-pointed needles, pair of size 5 US (3.75mm) straight needles • Waste yarn • Crochet hook • Tapestry needle • Stuffing • Samples knit with Cascade 220 (4/worsted weight; 100% wool; each approx 3½ oz/100g and 220 yds/201m) • 2 skeins 9461 (Lime Heather) • 1 skein 7826 (California Poppy) • <1 yard 8555 (Black)

FINISHED SIZE » Approx 9 inches wide, 5 inches tall, 6 inches deep

GAUGE » 2 inches = 11 stitches and 15½ rows in stockinette stitch (knit on RS, purl on WS)

Notes: Make sure your gauge for the stranded knitting sections and knitting with a single color are the same. Adjust your needle size for the stranded knitting sections, if necessary.

In pieces that incorporate the color pattern, the stitch count is always a multiple of 8, but row count isn't always a multiple of 6, so work rows of color pattern until you come to the end of the row count for that piece.

Base

Using provisional cast-on with waste yarn and a crochet hook, CO 38 sts of MC onto one dpn.

With MC, and beginning with a knit row, work 29 rows St st.

Pick up sts to work in a rnd

Instead of turning for the next purl row, rotate piece 90 degrees clockwise and use a second dpn to pick up and knit 22 sts along side of piece. "Unzip" waste yarn, slip the 38 sts onto a third needle, and knit. With a fourth needle, pick up and knit 22 sts along the remaining side (A, page 73).

Place marker. You will continue to knit these 120 sts in a rnd using a fifth needle.

Incorporating CC, knit 7 rnds in Color Pattern, using stranded color knitting technique.

Next rnd: With MC, k38, then BO remaining 88 sts, and BO the last st using first st of rnd. You will be left with one st on your right needle, and 37 on your left.

Knit to the end of the row, and turn.

Beginning with a purl row, work 27 rows St st.

BO all sts.

Couch Back

With MC and straight needles, CO 43 sts.

Beginning with a purl (WS) row, work Rows 1–56 as indicated in the Couch Back chart.

BO all sts.

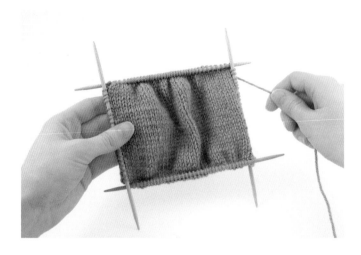

A Once you have knit 29 rows, pick up stitches on the other three sides and begin knitting in the round while incorporating the couch color pattern.

B Fold down the flap on the couch base so that it aligns with the bound-off edges, then use mattress stitch to close the seam.

Side Panels (MAKE 2)

With MC, CO 56 sts onto 3 dpns, place marker, and join in a rnd.

Knit 13 rnds in color pattern, then BO all sts with MC.

Bottom Cushions (MAKE 2)

With MC, CO 40 sts onto 3 dpns, place marker, and join in a rnd.

Knit 25 rnds in color pattern, then BO all sts with MC.

Top Cushions (MAKE 2)

With MC, CO 40 sts onto 3 dpns, place marker, and join in a rnd.

Knit 6 rnds in color pattern.

Next rnd: K20 as est, CO 8 using backward loop, k20 as est.

Knit 10 more rnds in color pattern, then BO all sts with MC.

Arm Rests (MAKE 2)

With MC, CO 4 sts onto one dpn.

Rnd 1 (work as I-cord): [Kfb] 4 times (8 sts).

Distribute sts onto 3 needles and place marker to continue to work in a rnd.

Rnd 2: [Kfb] 8 times (16 sts).

Rnd 3: Knit.

Rnd 4: [Kfb, k1] 8 times (24 sts).

Rnd 5: Knit.

Rnds 6–32: Knit 27 rnds in color pattern.

Switch to MC.

Rnd 33: [K2tog, k1] 8 times (16 sts).

Rnd 34: Knit.

Stuff piece before continuing.

Rnd 35: [K2tog] 8 times (8 sts).

Stuff end of piece, then break yarn and draw tightly through sts with tapestry needle.

Finishing

Sew flap on base using mattress stitch, and stuff lightly before closing up, so that the piece is filled out, but not puffy (B, above). The seamed side will become the bottom of the couch.

Fold couch back piece in two, and seam around the sides using mattress stitch, stuffing fully, but without over-stuffing, before closing up.

For top cushions, bottom cushions, and side panels, lay each piece flat and seam along open edges, and stuff before closing.

Embroider eyes with black yarn and tapestry needle. For each eye, use about 6 stitches across ½ knitted stitch in the center of cushion.

Assemble pieces as indicated in schematic.

Bottom and top cushions can either sit on couch unattached or be tacked on with a few sts for each. Weave in all loose ends.

COLOR PATTERN

Repeat every 8 sts in rnd

6

1

8   1

■ Knit with MC

■ Knit with CC

COUCH PIECES

Note: Arm rest and base are shown as stuffed and closed.

- - - - - Area to be seamed

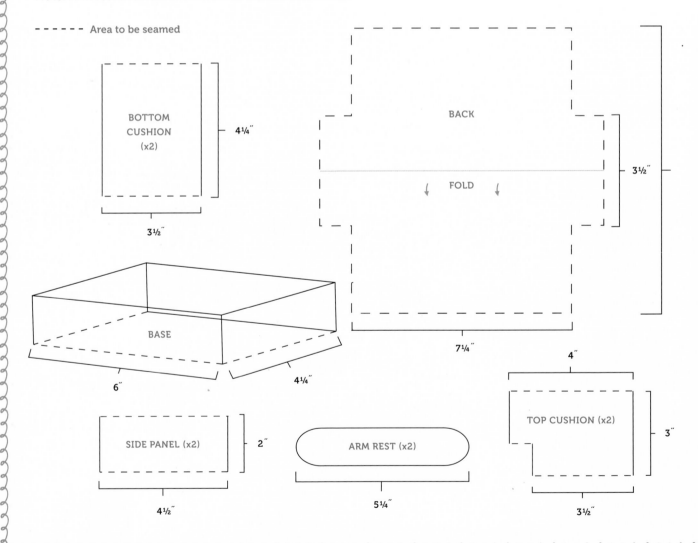

BOTTOM
CUSHION
(x2)

4¼″

3½″

BACK

FOLD

3½″

7¼″

4″

BASE

6″   4¼″

TOP CUSHION (x2)

3″

SIDE PANEL (x2)

2″

ARM REST (x2)

4½″   5¼″   3½″

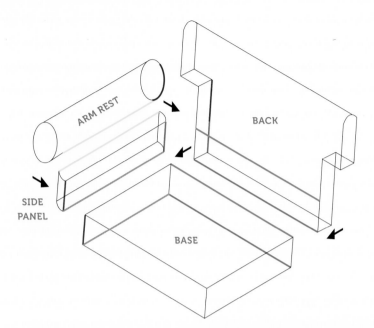

COUCH ASSEMBLY

Note: Only right side panel and arm rest are shown; mirror assembly shown for left side panel and arm rest.

Attach areas of same colors together using mattress stitch in the following order:

— Bottom of back to bottom of base
— Back to top of base where the two areas meet
— Side panel to side of base
— Front of side panel to front of base
— Back of side panel to back of base
— Arm rest to top of side panel
— Back side of arm rest to back where the two areas meet up

COUCH BACK

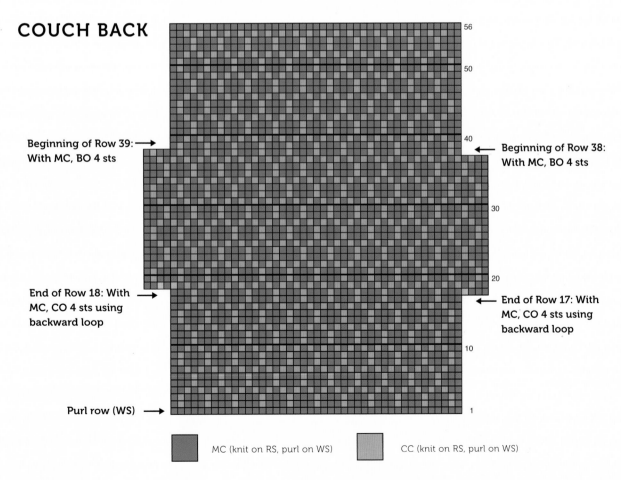

Beginning of Row 39: With MC, BO 4 sts

Beginning of Row 38: With MC, BO 4 sts

End of Row 18: With MC, CO 4 sts using backward loop

End of Row 17: With MC, CO 4 sts using backward loop

Purl row (WS) →

56
50
40
30
20
10
1

■ MC (knit on RS, purl on WS)   ■ CC (knit on RS, purl on WS)

TV GUY

No longer the center of attention, this old tube finally gets control of the remote. All the competitive ice skating he can watch!

TECHNIQUES » Provisional cast-on, intarsia, picking up sts, mattress stitch, k2tog, yo, I-cord

YOU'LL NEED » Worsted-weight yarn in 4 colors: main body color (Color 1), screen color (Color 2), accent color (Color 3), and antennae and cord/plug color (Color 4) • Set of 7-inch size 5 US (3.75mm) double-pointed needles Waste yarn • Crochet hook • Safety eyes (size 12mm) • Tapestry needle • Stuffing • **Samples knit with** Cascade 220 (4/worsted weight; 100% wool; each

approx 3½ oz/100g and 220 yds/201m) • 1 skein 9542 (Blaze) or 9421 (Blue Hawaii) • <1 skein 9402 (Dark Grey & Medium Grey Tweed) • <1 skein 8686 (Brown) or 8509 (Grey) • <1 skein 8555 (Black)

FINISHED SIZE » Approx 6⅓ inches tall (not including antennae) and 5 inches wide

GAUGE » 2 inches = 11 stitches and 15½ rows in stockinette stitch (knit on RS, purl on WS)

Screen

Before casting on, make a bobbin or small ball (about 3 yards) of Color 1 and set aside to use later.

Using provisional cast-on with waste yarn and a crochet hook, CO 26 sts onto one needle.

With Color 1, and beginning with a knit row, work 4 rows St st.

For Rows 5–22, incorporate Color 2 as indicated below, and use bobbin of Color 1 to work the smaller section of Color 1 (A, page 78).

Row 5: K7 Color 1, k15 Color 2, k4 Color 1 (from bobbin).

Row 6: P3 Color 1 (from bobbin), p17

Color 2, p6 Color 1.

Rows 7–21: Work 15 rows St st as est, finishing with a knit row.

Row 22: P4 Color 1, p15 Color 2, p7 Color 1.

Drop Color 2 and bobbin of Color 1, and continue to work only with main ball of Color 1.

Rows 23–27: Work 5 rows St st, finishing with a knit row.

Form Body

Instead of turning for the next purl row, rotate piece 90 degrees clockwise, and use a second needle to pick up and knit 18 sts along side of

MAKE ME FOR
Couch potatoes

piece. "Unzip" waste yarn, slip the 26 sts onto a third needle, and knit. With a fourth needle, pick up and knit 18 sts along the remaining side (B, page 78).

Place marker. You will continue to knit these 88 sts in a rnd using a fifth needle.

First rnd: K26, k18 tbl, k26, k18 tbl. Knit 23 rnds.

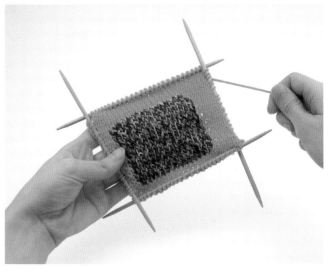

A Incorporate Color 2 for the TV's screen and the bobbin of Color 1 for the thinner section of orange, as shown from the back.

B Once the screen is complete, pick up stitches on the other three sides and begin knitting in the round.

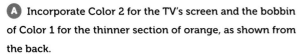

Next rnd: K26, then BO to end, and BO the last st using the first st of rnd. You will be left with one st on your right needle, and 25 on your left.

Continue to knit to the end of the row.

Turn, and beginning with a purl row, work 25 rows St st.

BO all sts.

Fold flap down to line up with BO edges, and begin sewing it down using mattress stitch (C, above right).

Before closing up, stuff piece fully, and attach eyes, placed in the vertical center of "screen" and spaced about 7 sts apart from each other.

Dials (MAKE 2)

With Color 3, CO 8 sts onto 3 needles, leaving a tail for seaming, and join in a rnd.

Rnd 1: [Kfb, k1] 4 times (12 sts).

Rnd 2: Knit.

Rnd 3: [K2tog] 6 times (6 sts).

Break yarn and draw tightly through sts with tapestry needle.

Legs (MAKE 4)

With Color 3, CO 20 sts onto 3 needles, leaving a long tail for seaming, and join in a rnd.

Rnds 1 and 2: Knit.

Rnd 3: [K2tog, k3] 4 times (16 sts).

Rnds 4 and 5: Knit.

Rnd 6: [K2tog, k2] 4 times (12 sts).

Rnds 7 and 8: Knit.

Rnd 9: [K2tog, k1] 4 times (8 sts).

Break yarn and draw tightly through sts with tapestry needle.

Antennae Dome

With Color 3, CO 30 sts onto 3 needles, leaving a long tail for seaming, and join in a rnd.

Rnds 1 and 2: Knit.

Rnd 3: [K2tog, k3] 6 times (24 sts).

Rnd 4: Knit.

Rnd 5: K2tog, k2, k2tog, yo, k2tog, [k2tog, k2] twice, k2tog, yo, [k2tog] twice, k2 (18 sts).

Rnd 6: Knit.

Rnd 7: [K2tog, k1] 6 times (12 sts).

Rnd 8: [K2tog] 6 times (6 sts).

Break yarn and draw tightly through sts with tapestry needle.

Antennae

With Color 4, CO 5 sts onto one needle, and knit I-cord until approx 6 inches long. Break yarn and draw tightly through sts with tapestry needle.

Cord

With Color 4, pick up and knit 4 sts at back of TV, about 10 sts from base of

C Fold down the flap so that it aligns with the bound-off edges at the back, then use mattress stitch to close the seam.

TV, and about 8 sts from left side of TV. Pick up using bars between knitted sts so that they are close together. Knit I-cord until approx 3 inches long, then continue to knit in a rnd as follows.

Rnd 1: [Kfb] 4 times, and distribute 8 sts onto 3 needles.

Rnd 2: [Kfb] 8 times (16 sts).

Rnds 3–5: Knit.

Stuff before continuing.

Rnd 6: [K2tog] 8 times (8 sts).

Break yarn and draw tightly through sts.

For prongs, CO 2 sts onto one needle, and knit an I-cord until approx 1½ inches long. Thread through end of plug to form two prongs that are parallel to each other.

Finishing

Lightly stuff dials, and attach to the right of screen using mattress stitch.

Thread antennae through the holes you created in the antennae dome with the yarn overs. (It should fit snugly.) Lightly stuff dome, and attach to top middle of TV using mattress stitch.

Stuff feet firmly and attach to four corners of base of TV using mattress stitch.

Weave in all loose ends.

CUTER POLLUTERS

Who says pollution has to be bad and scary?
(Everyone does.)

TECHNIQUES » Kfb, k2tog, mattress stitch

YOU'LL NEED » Worsted-weight yarn in gray (MC), contrasting color for smoke (CC), and small amount of black • Set of 5-inch size 6 US (4.0mm) double-pointed needles • Two sets of safety eyes (size 9mm) • Tapestry needle • Stuffing • **Samples knit with** Cascade 220 (4/worsted weight; 100% wool; each approx 3½ oz/100g and 220 yds/201m) • 1 skein 8509 (Grey) • <1 skein each 7809 (Violet), 9461 (Lime Heather), 7821 (Sienna) • <1 skein 8555 (Black)

FINISHED SIZE » Approx 7½ inches tall

GAUGE » 2 inches = 10 stitches and 14 rows in stockinette stitch (knit on RS, purl on WS)

Body and smoke

With MC, CO 4 sts onto one needle.

Rnd 1 (work as I-cord): [Kfb] 4 times (8 sts).

Distribute sts onto 3 needles, place marker, and join in a rnd.

Rnd 2: [Kfb] 8 times (16 sts).

Rnd 3: Knit.

Rnd 4: [Kfb, k1] 8 times (24 sts).

Rnd 5: Knit.

Rnd 6: [Kfb, k2] 8 times (32 sts).

Rnds 7–28: Knit 22 rnds.

Rnd 29: [K2tog, k6] 4 times (28 sts).

Rnds 30–33: Knit 4 rnds.

Rnd 34: [K2tog, k5] 4 times (24 sts).

Rnd 35: Knit.

Stuff piece so far.

Break yarn, leaving a long tail (about 20 inches) on the outside of your knitting.

Switch to CC.

Rnd 36: [K2tog, k4] (20 sts).

Rnd 37: Knit.

Rnd 38: [K2tog, k3] (16 sts).

Rnds 39–42: Knit 4 rnds.

Rnd 43: K1, [kfb] 3 times, k1, [kfb] twice, k2, [kfb] twice, k1, [kfb] 3 times, k1 (26 sts).

Even rnds 44–74: Knit.

Rnd 45: K1, [kfb] twice, k to last 3 sts, [kfb] twice, k1 (30 sts).

Rnd 47: K1, kfb, k to last 2 sts, kfb, k1 (32 sts).

Rnd 49: K1, [k2tog] 3 times, k4, [k2tog] twice, k2, [k2tog] twice, k4, [k2tog] 3 times, k1 (22 sts).

Rnd 51: K1, [kfb] 3 times, [k2tog] 3 times, k2, [k2tog] 3 times, [kfb] 3 times, k1 (22 sts).

Rnd 53: K1, [kfb] twice, k5, [kfb] twice, k2, [kfb] twice, k5, [kfb] twice, k1 (30 sts).

Rnd 55: K1, kfb, k to last 2 sts, kfb, k1 (32 sts).

MAKE US FOR *Grim greenies*

A Fold the smoke section down into the chimney to hide the color change and make it look like the smoke is coming out of the chimney.

B Sew around the rim of the chimney, making your stitches invisible by stitching vertically between the knitted stitches.

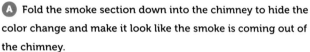

Rnd 57: K1, kfb, k to last 2 sts, kfb, k1 (34 sts).

Rnd 59: K1, [k2tog] 3 times, k5, [k2tog] twice, k2, [k2tog] twice, k5, [k2tog] 3 times, k1 (24 sts).

Rnd 61: K1, [kfb] 3 times, k1, [k2tog] 3 times, k2, [k2tog] 3 times, k1, [kfb] 3 times, k1 (24 sts).

Rnd 63: K1, [kfb] twice, k6, [kfb] twice, k2, [kfb] twice, k6, [kfb] twice, k1 (32 sts).

Rnd 65: K1, kfb, k to last 2 sts, kfb, k1 (34 sts).

Rnd 67: Work same as Rnd 65 (36 sts).

Rnd 69: K13, [k2tog] twice, k2, [k2tog] twice, k13 (32 sts).

Rnd 71: K1, k2tog, k8, [k2tog] twice, k2, [k2tog] twice, k8, k2tog, k1 (26 sts).

Rnd 73: K1, k2tog, k5, [k2tog] twice, k2, [k2tog] twice, k5, k2tog, k1 (20 sts).

After finishing Rnd 74, lay piece flat, so that beginning of rnds is on the right side. The side facing up will be the front of the piece. Making note of where the front is, reach down into piece and attach eyes to chimney section, placed about 13 sts up from the last increase rnd and spaced about 5 sts apart from each other.

Stuff the rest of the piece fully without over-stuffing, then attach eyes to the top of smoke section, spaced about 4 sts apart from each other.

Continue as follows to finish.

Rnd 75: K1, [k2tog] 4 times, k2, [k2tog] 4 times, k1 (12 sts).

Rnd 76: [K2tog] 6 times (6 sts).

Add a little more stuffing to the top, then break yarn and draw tightly through sts with tapestry needle.

Arms (MAKE 2)

With MC, CO 6 sts onto 3 needles, leaving a tail for seaming, and join in a rnd.

Rnd 1: K1, [kfb] twice, k1, [kfb] twice (10 sts).

Rnds 2–7: Knit 6 rnds.

Stuff before continuing.

Rnd 8: K1, [k2tog] twice, k1, [k2tog] twice (6 sts).

Break yarn and draw tightly through sts with tapestry needle.

Feet (MAKE 2)

With MC, CO 6 sts onto 3 needles, leaving a tail for seaming, and join in a rnd.

Rnd 1: [Kfb] 6 times (12 sts).

Rnd 2: Knit.

Rnd 3: K4, [kfb] 4 times, k4 (16 sts).

Rnds 4–9: Knit 6 rnds.

Rnd 10: K4, [k2tog] 4 times, k4 (12 sts).

Stuff before continuing.

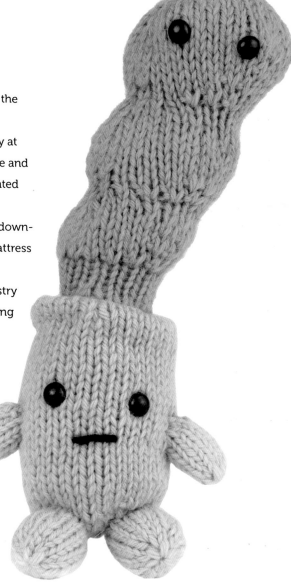

ⓒ Attach feet to base of body at an angle, with toes pointed out.

Rnd 11: [K2tog] 6 times (6 sts).

Break yarn and draw tightly through sts with tapestry needle.

Finishing

Fold bottom part of smoke down into chimney and fold top of chimney up to form a rim, so that the place where you switched colors is hidden when you look at the piece straight on (A, opposite, far left).

Using a tapestry needle and the long tail of MC that you left when changing colors, sew around the two layers of the rim to secure it in place. Make your stitches on the outside of the piece run vertically alongside the knitted sts, so that they are invisible (B, opposite, near left).

You may need to massage some of the stuffing around to make the fold between the chimney and the smoke stay in place and also to keep the smoke upright.

Attach feet to base of body at an angle using tapestry needle and mattress stitch, with toes pointed outward (C, above).

Attach arms to sides at a downward-pointed angle using mattress stitch.

With black yarn and tapestry needle, embroider mouth using backstitch.

Weave in all loose ends.

MAKE US FOR
Urban aspirants
and refugees

SHYSCRAPERS »

Even imposing high rises need a break from the big scary city sometimes.

TECHNIQUES » Provisional cast-on, picking up stitches, stranded color knitting, mattress stitch
YOU'LL NEED » Worsted-weight yarn in 3 building colors (MC), yellow (CC), and gray • Set of 5-inch size 5 US (3.75mm) double-pointed needles, one 32-inch size 5 US (3.75mm) circular needle • Waste yarn • Crochet hook • 7 sets of safety eyes (size 9mm) • Stuffing • **Samples knit with** Cascade 220 (4/worsted weight; 100% wool;

each approx 3½ oz/100g and 220 yds/201m) • 1 skein each 9421 (Blue Hawaii), 7808 (Purple Hyacinth), 9469 (Hot Pink), 7827 (Goldenrod), and 8401 (Silver Grey)
FINISHED SIZE » Base approx 10 inches long by 5 inches wide; building heights range from 2½ inches to 5½ inches tall (including antenna)
GAUGE » 2 inches = 11 stitches and 15½ rows in stockinette stitch (knit on RS, purl on WS)

Notes: Buildings are worked from the top down.

The window chart is written with all windows filled in, or "lit," using CC. If desired, rather than follow the pattern as written for each window, replace CC with MC for some sections to result in blank, or "unlit" windows, as shown in photos of the finished project.

The base is written using the magic loop method of knitting with a circular needle (page 40). If you prefer to use double-pointed needles, you can use one set of 7-inch size 5 US (3.75mm) double-pointed needles instead.

Building 1: NARROW BUILDING

Using provisional cast-on with waste yarn and a crochet hook, CO 7 sts onto one dpn.

With MC, and beginning with a knit row, work 9 rows St st (see photo, page 86).

Instead of turning for the next purl row, rotate piece 90 degrees clockwise, and use a second dpn to pick up and knit 5 sts along side of piece. "Unzip" waste yarn, slip the 7 sts onto a third needle, and knit. With a fourth needle, pick up and knit 5 sts along the remaining side. You should have 24 sts on your needles.

Distribute sts onto 3 needles and

place marker. You will continue to knit the rest of the building in a rnd.

Begin window pattern, and repeat to make your building as tall as you like, with as many rows of windows as you like.

Once you have finished your bottommost window, knit three more rnds of MC.

BO all sts.

Antenna (OPTIONAL)

With MC and dpns, CO 3 sts onto one needle to work as I-cord.

Work 6 rows of I-cord, then break yarn and draw tightly through sts with tapestry needle. Stitch to top of building.

After working 9 rows in stockinette stitch, pick up stitches on the other three sides of the piece and begin knitting in the round.

Building 2: WIDE BUILDING

Using provisional cast-on with waste yarn and a crochet hook, CO 7 sts onto one dpn.

With MC, and beginning with a knit row, work 11 rows St st.

Instead of turning for the next purl row, rotate piece 90 degrees clockwise, and use a second dpn to pick up and knit 8 sts along side of piece. "Unzip" waste yarn, and slip the 7 sts onto a third needle, and knit. With a fourth needle, pick up and knit 8 sts along the remaining side. You should have 30 sts on your needles.

Distribute sts onto 3 needles and place marker. You will continue to knit the rest of the building in a rnd.

Begin window pattern, and repeat to make your building as tall as you like, with as many rows of windows as you like.

Once you have finished your bottommost window, knit three more rnds of MC.

BO all sts.

Building 3: LANDMARK BUILDING

With MC, CO 3 sts onto one dpn. Work 6 rows of I-cord.

Next rnd (work as I-cord): [Kfb] 3 times (6 sts).

Distribute 6 sts onto 3 needles and join in a rnd.

Rnd 1: [Kfb] 6 times (12 sts). Place marker.
Rnd 2: [K1MC, k1CC] 6 times.
Rnd 3 (work in MC): Kfb, k4, [kfb] twice, k4, kfb (16 sts).
Rnd 4: [K1MC, k1CC] 8 times.
Rnd 5 (work in MC): Kfb, k6, [kfb] twice, k6, kfb (20 sts).
Rnd 6: [K1MC, k1CC] 10 times.

Rnd 7 (work in MC): Kfb, k8, [kfb] twice, k8, kfb (24 sts).
Rnd 8: [K1MC, K1CC] 12 times.
Rnd 9: Knit in MC.

Begin window pattern, and repeat to make your building as tall as you like, with as many rows of windows as you like.

Once you have finished your bottommost window, knit three more rnds of MC.

BO all sts.

Base

With gray yarn and circular needle, CO 60 sts and join in a rnd using the magic loop method.

Knit 82 rnds, then BO all sts.

Finishing

Lay base flat, and sew up one end using tapestry needle and mattress stitch. Stuff fully without over-stuffing, and sew up the other end.

Attach eyes to buildings, and stuff each building.

Attach buildings to base using mattress stitch, turning a 90-degree corner when you reach the end of each building side. Refer to schematic for placement.

For dashed "street" lines, cut a long piece of yellow yarn, and with tapestry needle, embroider onto perimeter of base using a running stitch, slipping your needle under and over every three knit sts on the base.

Weave in all loose ends.

WINDOW PATTERN

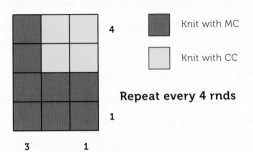

Knit with MC

Knit with CC

Repeat every 4 rnds

Repeat every 3 sts in rnd

The color chart is written with all windows filled in, or "lit," using CC. If desired, rather than follow the pattern as written for each window, replace CC with MC for some sections to result in blank, or "unlit" windows, as shown in photos of the finished project.

BUILDING PLACEMENT

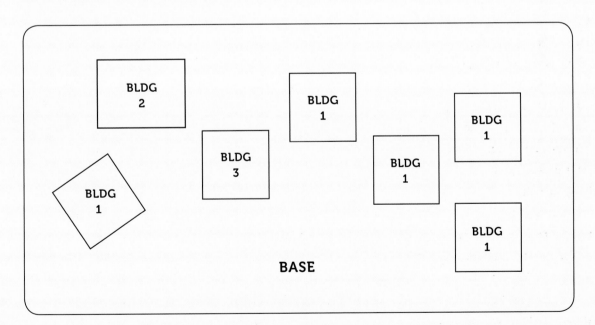

impractical
WEARABLES

Go fashion-forward with wearable toys.
They're all the rage in Milan, you know.

Pocket Protectors   »   Neck Nuzzler   »   Love Muff   »   Feet Eaters

Naughty and Nicey

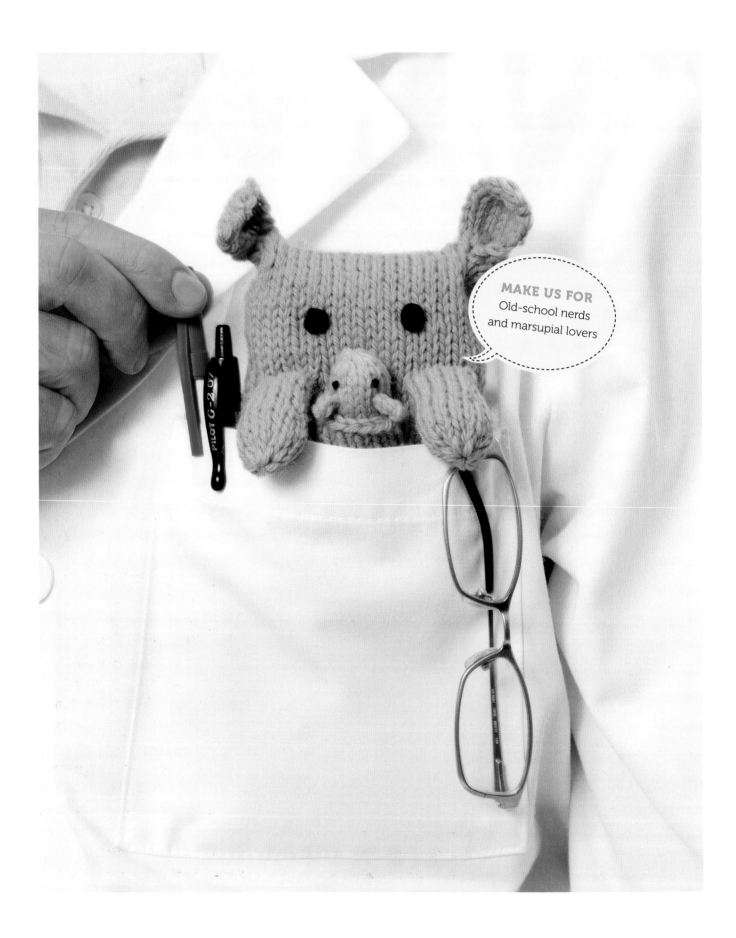

MAKE US FOR
Old-school nerds
and marsupial lovers

POCKET PROTECTORS

Their mission: to keep extraneous keys and wallets from entering your pocket! (But really they just want a free ride.)

TECHNIQUES » Kfb, k2tog, k3tog, p2tog, backward loop cast-on, mattress stitch, I-cord
YOU'LL NEED » Worsted-weight yarn in 2 colors and black • Set of 6-inch size 6 US (4.0mm) double-pointed needles, set of 5-inch size 5 US (3.75mm) double-pointed needles • Stitch holder • Tapestry needle • Stuffing • Samples knit with Cascade 220 (4/worsted weight; 100% wool; each approx 3½ oz/100g and 220 yds/201m)

• 1 skein 8905 (Robin Egg Blue) • <1 skein 7827 (Goldenrod) • <1 yard 8555 (Black)
FINISHED SIZE » Parent protector approx 5 inches tall by 3½ inches wide; baby protector approx 1¼ inches tall
GAUGE FOR LARGER NEEDLES » 2 inches = 10 stitches and 14 rows in stockinette stitch (knit on RS, purl on WS)

Note: Baby Protector is very small and not suitable for small children.

Parent Protector Feet

CO 6 sts onto 3 larger needles and join in a rnd.
Rnd 1: [Kfb] 6 times (12 sts).
Rnd 2: Knit.
Rnd 3: [Kfb, k4, kfb] twice (16 sts).
Rnds 4 and 5: Knit.

Break yarn, and place these 16 sts onto a holder.

Repeat Rnds 1–5 above to make another foot, without breaking yarn.
Join feet together
K8, and CO 5 sts using backward loop method. Place remaining 8

unworked sts onto one needle to work later. Slip 16 sts from holder onto two more needles, and with a fifth needle, K16. CO 5 sts using backward loop, then knit the remaining 8 sts from your second foot (42 sts).

Distribute sts onto 3 needles, and place marker. You will continue to work in a rnd to form the body.

Body

Rnds 1–38: Knit.
Row 39: K4, BO 13, k7. You should have 8 sts on your right needle (beginning after the section you just bound off). Slip the other 21 live sts onto one needle to work later.

Row 40: Turn and k8 (on what was until now the WS).
Rows 41–46: Beginning with a purl row, work 6 rows St st.
Row 47: P1, [p2tog] 3 times, p1 (5 sts).
Row 48: K1, k3tog, k1 (3 sts).

Break yarn and draw tightly through sts with tapestry needle.

Reattach yarn to next live stitch, to the immediate left of the ear you just formed.
Next row: BO 13, k7. You should again have 8 sts on your needle.

Repeat Rows 40–48 above to form a second ear.

Break yarn and draw tightly through sts with tapestry needle.

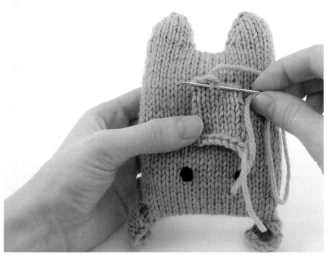

A When seaming the top of the Parent Protector's head, fold the ears inward toward the knit side.

B Begin about 7 stitches up from the seam between the feet to attach the bottom of the pocket first using mattress stitch.

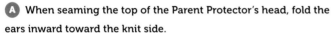

Pocket

CO 8 sts onto one larger needle using backward loop method, leaving a 15-inch tail for seaming.

Beginning with a knit row, work 10 rows St st.

BO all sts.

Arms (MAKE 2)

CO 10 sts onto 3 larger needles using backward loop method, leaving a tail for seaming, and join in a rnd.

Rnds 1 and 2: Knit.

Rnd 3: Kfb, k4, kfb, k4 (12 sts).

Rnds 4–7: Knit 4 rnds.

Rnd 8: Kfb, k5, kfb, k5 (14 sts).

Rnds 9–12: Knit 4 rnds.

Rnd 13: [K2tog] 7 times (7 sts).

Break yarn and draw tightly through sts with tapestry needle.

Finishing

Sew up gap between feet using tapestry needle and mattress stitch. Stuff body without over-stuffing, so that it is relatively flat. Sew up the two BO edges at top of head with mattress stitch, allowing the ears to fold inward toward their knit sides (A, above).

With black yarn and a tapestry needle, embroider on eyes, making 6 horizontal stitches across one knitted st for each eye and space them about 6 sts apart.

Use mattress stitch to attach bottom (CO) edge of pocket to body about 7 sts above seam between feet (B, above).

Fold pocket up against the body, and attach sides of pocket using mattress stitch (C, above right).

Stuff arms, and using mattress stitch, attach them just above and to either side of pocket, at a downward angle so that they lie nearly flat against the body (D, above right).

Weave in all loose ends.

Baby Protector

CO 6 sts onto 3 smaller needles and join in a rnd.

Rnd 1: [Kfb] 6 times (12 sts).

Rnds 2–11: Knit.

Rnd 12: [K2tog] 6 times (6 sts).

Stuff piece, break yarn and draw tightly through sts with tapestry needle.

With black yarn and a tapestry needle, embroider on eyes, with one horizontal stitch across ½ knitted st.

For arms, CO 2 sts onto one needle and knit an I-cord until approx 1¼ inches long. With tapestry needle, thread one end of it through body, just under one eye, and back out again under the other eye to form two arms.

Weave in all loose ends.

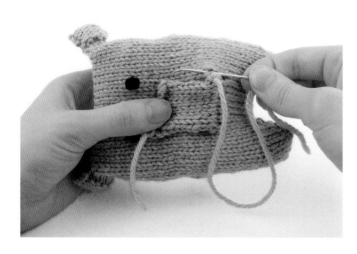

C After attaching the bottom of the pocket, attach the sides to the body using mattress stitch.

D Attach Parent Protector's arms at a downward-pointing angle.

MAKE THEM FOR Tempted Timmys and Indecisive Ingrids (and only people with those names, mind you!)

NAUGHTY AND NICEY

Externalize your inner conflicts with these guys and you'll have someone else to blame for those extra inches.

TECHNIQUES » Kfb, k2tog, I-cord, backward loop cast on, mattress stitch

YOU'LL NEED » Worsted-weight yarn in white (MC), red (MC), yellow (CC), and black (CC) • Set of 7-inch size 6 US (4.0mm) double-pointed needles, set of 7-inch size 5 US (3.75mm) double-pointed needles • Safety eyes (9mm) • Stuffing • **Samples knit with** Cascade 220 (4/worsted weight; 100% wool; each approx 3½ oz/100g and 220 yds/201m) • 1 skein each 8505 (White) and 2413 (Red) • <1 skein each 7827 (Goldenrod) and 8555 (Black)

FINISHED SIZE » Angel/devil approx 3½ inches tall Shoulder strap, measured around top of shoulder and under armpit: S (13–15 inches) (M [16–18 inches], L [19–21 inches])

GAUGE FOR LARGER NEEDLES (ANGEL AND DEVIL) » 2 inches = 10 stitches and 14 rows in stockinette stitch (knit on RS, purl on WS)

GAUGE FOR SMALLER NEEDLES (SHOULDER STRAP) » 4 inches = 26 stitches in k2, p2 rib when unstretched and 20 sts when lightly stretched.

Body
(SAME FOR ANGEL AND DEVIL)

With MC, CO 4 sts onto one larger needle.

Rnd 1 (work as I-cord): [Kfb] 4 times (8 sts).

Distribute sts onto 3 needles, place marker, and join in a rnd.

Rnd 2: [Kfb] 8 times (16 sts).

Odd rnds 3–11: Knit.

Rnd 4: [Kfb, k1] 8 times (24 sts).

Rnd 6: [Kfb, k2] 8 times (32 sts).

Rnd 8: [Kfb, k3] 8 times (40 sts).

Rnd 10: [Kfb, k4] 8 times (48 sts).

Rnd 12: [Kfb, k5] 8 times (56 sts).

Rnds 13–18: Knit 6 rnds.

Rnd 19: [K2tog, k6] 7 times (49 sts).

Rnds 20–22: Knit.

Rnd 23: [K2tog, k5] 7 times (42 sts).

Rnds 24–26: Knit.

Rnd 27: [K2tog, k4] 7 times (35 sts).

Rnds 28 and 29: Knit.

Rnd 30: [K2tog, k3] 7 times (28 sts).

Rnd 31: Knit.

Rnd 32: [K2tog, k2] 7 times (21 sts).

Rnd 33: Knit.

Stuff before continuing.

Rnd 34: [K2tog, k1] 7 times (14 sts).

Rnd 35: [K2tog] 7 times (7 sts).

Attach eyes halfway down the body, spaced about 8 sts apart from each other.

Add a little more stuffing to the top of piece, then break yarn and draw tightly through sts with tapestry needle.

Arms and Legs

With MC and larger needle, pick up and knit 4 sts, picking up bars between knitted sts so that they are close together (A, page 96, top left).

Arms should be placed just under and about 4 sts to the outside of eyes.

Legs should be placed at the

A Pick up and knit 4 stitches for each arm, picking them up just under and 4 stitches outside of eyes.

B Pick up and knit 4 stitches for each leg, picking them up at the second-to-last increase round on the body and directly under the eyes.

second-to-last increase rnd on body, directly under eyes (B, above).

Rnds 1–6: Knit 6 rows of I-cord.

Rnd 7: Switch to CC and work one row of I-cord.

Rnd 8: [Kfb] 4 times (8 sts).

Distribute 8 sts onto 3 needles to continue to work in a rnd.

Rnd 9: [Kfb] 8 times (16 sts).

Rnds 10–12: Knit.

Rnd 13: [K2tog] 8 times (8 sts).

Stuff piece, then break yarn and draw tightly through sts.

Devil's Horns/ Angel's Wings

With CC, CO 6 sts onto 3 larger needles, leaving a long tail for seaming, and join in a rnd.

Rnd 1: [Kfb] 6 times (12 sts).

Rnds 2 and 3: Knit.

Rnd 4: K2tog, k to last 2 sts, k2tog (10 sts)

Rnds 5 and 6: Same as Rnd 4 (6 sts).

Rnd 7: Knit.

Without stuffing piece, break yarn and draw tightly through sts.

Devil's Tail

With MC and larger needle, pick up 4 sts on backside of body. Work same as arms and legs, but immediately before closing off, knit two additional rnds.

Angel's Halo

With CC, CO 40 sts onto 3 larger needles and join in a rnd.

Knit 4 rnds, then BO all sts.

Shoulder Strap

Sizes S (M, L)

With CC and smaller needles, CO 8 sts onto one needle to work straight.

Row 1: Purl.

Row 2: [Kfb] twice, k to last 2 sts, [kfb] twice (12 sts).

Row 3: Purl.

Row 4: Same as Row 2 (16 sts).

Without turning, CO 62 (70, 78) sts using backwards loop method. Being careful not to twist your sts, join with the first st of 16. This join will become the beginning of the rnd.

Rnds 5–11: K16, [K2, p2] to last 2 sts, k2.

Rnd 12: K16, and loosely BO 61 (69, 77) sts as est, leaving one st on the right needle before you begin the next row.

You will continue to work the remaining sts straight on one needle.

Row 13: K2tog, pass over last st from previous rnd to BO, k2tog, k8, [k2tog] twice (12 sts).

Row 14: Purl.

C Attach the flat section of the shoulder strap to the base of the body using backstitch, with the knit sides facing each other.

Row 15: [K2tog] twice, k4, [k2tog] twice
(8 sts).
Row 16: Purl.
    BO all sts.

Finishing

Attach horns to devil body with pointed ends up. Attach wings to angel body a bit lower down, with pointed ends down. Fold angel's halo over (knit side out) and sew the CO and BO edges together using mattress stitch. Tack it to the back of angel's head with a few small sts.

Attach base of body to flat part of shoulder strap, with the purl sts on the strap against the bottom of the body (C, above). Sew around the perimeter of the flat area using backstitch.

Weave in all loose ends.

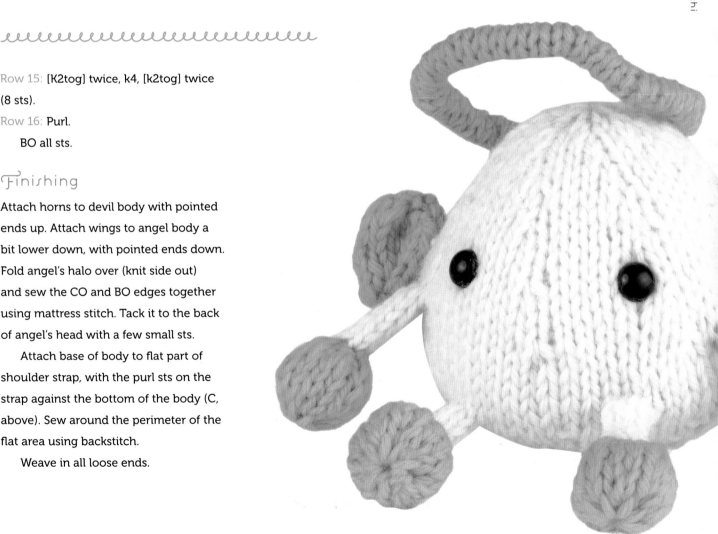

MAKE ME FOR
Serious snugglers and
hard-core huggers

NECK NUZZLER

This darling bunny may look like an innocent accessory, but watch out—she's a chronic eavesdropper.

TECHNIQUES » Kfb, k2tog, ssk, picking up stitches, I-cord, duplicate stitch
YOU'LL NEED » Worsted-weight yarn in gray (MC) and pink (CC) • Set of 5-inch size 5 US (3.75mm) double-pointed needles • Stitch holder • Safety eyes (size 9mm) • Tapestry needle • Stuffing • **Samples knit with** Cascade 220 (4/worsted weight; 100% wool; each

approx 3½ oz/100g and 220 yds/201m) • 1 skein 8509 (Grey) • <1 skein 9477 (Tutu)
FINISHED SIZE » Body approx 3 inches tall; ears approx 6¼ inches long, not including I-cord
GAUGE » 2 inches = 11 stitches and 15½ rows in stockinette stitch (knit on RS, purl on WS)

Note: Pattern is written in one size. For a different length, lengthen or shorten I-cord as needed when knitting, or simply tie I-cord lower or higher in back.

Feet

With MC, CO 6 sts onto 3 needles and join in a rnd.
Rnd 1: [Kfb] 6 times (12 sts). Place marker.
Rnds 2–5: Knit 4 rnds.
    Break yarn, and place these 12 sts onto a holder.
    Repeat Rnds 1–5 above to make another foot, without breaking yarn.
Join feet together
K6, and place remaining 6 unworked sts onto one needle to work later. Slip 12 sts from holder back onto needles,

and k12. Knit the remaining 6 sts from your second foot (24 sts).
    Distribute sts onto 3 needles, and place marker. You will continue to work in a rnd to form the body.

Body

Rnd 1: Kfb, k3, kfb, k2, kfb, k3, kfb, k12 (28 sts).
Even rnds 2–6: Knit.
Rnd 3: Kfb, k4, kfb, k4, kfb, k4, kfb, k12 (32 sts).
Rnd 5: Kfb, k5, kfb, k6, kfb, k5, kfb, k12 (36 sts).
Rnd 7: Kfb, k6, kfb, k8, kfb, k6, kfb, k12 (40 sts).
Rnds 8–11: Knit 4 rnds.
Rnd 12: K2tog, k6, k2tog, k8, ssk, k6, ssk, k12 (36 sts).

Odd rnds 13–21: Knit.
Rnd 14: K2tog, k5, k2tog, k6, ssk, k5, ssk, k12 (32 sts).
Rnd 16: K2tog, k4, k2tog, k4, ssk, k4, ssk, k12 (28 sts).
Rnd 18: k2tog, k3, k2tog, k2, ssk, k3, ssk, k12 (24 sts).
Rnd 20: [K2tog, k2] 6 times (18 sts).
    Stuff before continuing.
Rnd 22: [K2tog, k1] 6 times (12 sts).
Rnd 23: [K2tog] 6 times (6 sts).
    Attach eyes, placed about 9 sts from top of head, and spaced about 7 sts apart from each other. Break yarn and draw tightly through sts with tapestry needle.

Arms (MAKE 2)

Turn body upside down, and pick up

Ⓐ Turn the body upside down, and pick up and knit 3 stitches for the arm.

Ⓑ For the left ear, pick up and knit 10 stitches along the back side of the decrease seam.

and knit 3 sts just below and to the outside of eye (A, above left).

Row 1 (work as I-cord): [Kfb] 3 times (6 sts).

Distribute sts onto three needles and join in a rnd.

Rnds 2–4: Knit.

Break yarn and draw tightly through sts with tapestry needle (without stuffing arm).

Left Ear (BUNNY'S LEFT)

Pick up and knit 10 sts down along the back side of the decrease seam that appears on the left side of the head, beginning about 3 sts from top of head (B, above right).

Turn, and with a second needle, pick up and knit 10 sts along the front side of the seam (C, opposite, near right).

Distribute these 20 sts onto 3 needles, place marker, and continue to

knit in the rnd.

Rnds 1–33: Knit.

Rnd 34: K8, [k2tog] twice, k8 (18 sts).

Rnds 35–38: Knit 4 rnds.

Rnd 39: K7, [k2tog] twice, k7 (16 sts).

Rnds 40–43: Knit 4 rnds.

Rnd 44: K6, [k2tog] twice, k6 (14 sts).

Rnds 45–48: Knit 4 rnds.

Rnd 49: K5, [k2tog] twice, k5 (12 sts).

Rnds 50 and 51: Knit.

Rnd 52: [K2tog] 6 times (6 sts).

Place 6 sts onto one needle to work as I-cord.

Rnd 53: K1, [k2tog] twice, k1 (4 sts). With these 4 sts, make I-cord until approx 7½ inches long, or until desired length.

Right Ear (BUNNY'S RIGHT)

Pick up and knit 10 sts down along the front side of the decrease seam that appears on the right side of the head,

beginning about 3 sts from top of head. Turn, and with a second needle, pick up and knit 10 sts back up along the back of seam.

Distribute sts onto 3 needles, place marker, and work same as left ear, beginning with 33 knit rounds.

Finishing

Sew up gap between bunny's feet with a few stitches.

With CC and tapestry needle, embroider on nose with two sts, one long horizontal stitch across three sts, and one short vertical stitch to pull down horizontal st to a point (D, opposite, far right).

With CC and tapestry needle, use duplicate stitch to add patches to ears (E, opposite, bottom).

Weave in all loose ends.

C After picking up 10 stitches for the left ear, turn the piece and pick up 10 more stitches.

D For the nose, use a contrasting yarn to embroider one long horizontal stitch, then make one short vertical stitch to pull the horizontal stitch down to a point.

E Add patches to the ears using duplicate stitch.

DUPLICATE STITCH PATTERN

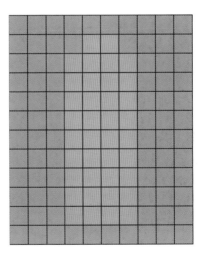

—— Base of ear

MAKE ME FOR
Vintage-style
fashionistas

LOVE MUFF

This muff is so stylish and warm, you just might want to share her! (She will tolerate such nonsense for short periods.)

TECHNIQUES » K2tog, mattress stitch

YOU'LL NEED » Worsted-weight yarn in dark pink (MC) and light pink (CC), and chunky yarn in blue • 2 circular needles: 32-inch size 6 US (4.0mm) and 32-inch size 8 US (5.0mm) • Set of 6-inch size 6 US (4.0mm) double-pointed needles • Stitch holder • 2 buttons (¾-inch diameter) • Tapestry needle • Sewing needle and embroidery thread (for attaching buttons) • Stuffing • **Samples knit with** Cascade 220 (4/worsted weight; 100% wool; each approx 3½ oz/100g and 220 yds/201m) • 1 skein each 7802 (Cerise) and 9478 (Cotton Candy) • Rowan Big Wool (6/super bulky; 100% wool; each approx 3½ oz/100g and 87 yds/80m) • 2 skeins 021 (Ice Blue)

FINISHED SIZE » Approx 9½ inches wide

GAUGE FOR BODY » 2 inches = 10 stitches and 14 rows in stockinette stitch (knit on RS, purl on WS)

GAUGE FOR LINING » 4 inches = 14 stitches and 18 rows in stockinette stitch

Note: Instead of using magic loop method of circular knitting for this pattern, you can also use sets of 7-inch double-pointed needles, if you prefer.

Body

With MC, CO 60 sts onto smaller circular needle, leaving a long tail for seaming. Place marker, and join in a rnd using the magic loop method.

Rnd 1: [Kfb, k2] to end (80 sts).

Rnd 2: Knit.

Rnd 3: [Kfb, k3] to end (100 sts).

Rnds 4–9: Knit 6 rnds.

Begin stripe pattern

Switch to CC, and knit 4 rnds.

Switch to MC, and knit 4 rnds.

Continue to alternate 4 rnds of CC and 4 rnds of MC until you have completed 9 total stripes of CC.

Switch to MC.

Rnds 78–83: Knit 6 rnds.

Rnd 84: [K2tog, k3] to end (80 sts).

Rnd 85: Knit.

Rnd 86: [K2tog, k2] to end (60 sts).

Rnd 87: Knit.

BO all sts, leaving a long tail for seaming.

Lining

With chunky yarn, CO 50 sts onto larger circular needle, place marker, and join in a rnd.

Knit until piece is ½ inch shorter than the body, or about 60 rnds.

Feet (MAKE 4)

With MC, CO 36 sts onto 3 dpns, leaving a long tail for seaming. Place marker, and join in a rnd.

Rnd 1: [Kfb, k5] 6 times (42 sts).

Rnds 2–8: Knit 7 rnds.

Rnd 9: [K2tog, k5] 6 times (36 sts).

Even rnds 10–16: Knit.

Rnd 11: [K2tog, k4] 6 times (30 sts).

Rnd 13: [K2tog, k3] 6 times (24 sts).

Rnd 15: [K2tog, k2] 6 times (18 sts).

Rnd 17: [K2tog, k1] 6 times (12 sts).

Break yarn and draw tightly through sts with tapestry needle.

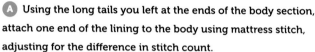

A Using the long tails you left at the ends of the body section, attach one end of the lining to the body using mattress stitch, adjusting for the difference in stitch count.

B Attach the feet to the bottom of the body, with the back two feet spaced wider apart than the front two feet.

Horns (MAKE 2)

With CC, CO 16 sts onto 3 dpns, leaving a tail for seaming, and join in a rnd.

Rnds 1–8: Knit.

Rnd 9: [Kfb] twice, k4, [kfb] 4 times, k4, [kfb] twice (24 sts).

Rnd 10: K6, place next 12 sts on holder to work later, k6.

Distribute the 12 working sts onto 3 needles to work in a rnd.

Rnd 11: Kfb, k3, [k2tog] twice, k3, kfb (12 sts).

Rnds 12–16: Knit 5 rnds.

Rnd 17: [K2tog] 6 times (6 sts).

Break yarn and draw tightly through sts with tapestry needle.

Place 12 sts from holder onto 3 needles, reattach yarn to last st, and join in a rnd.

Rnd 18: Knit.

Rnd 19: K2tog, k3, [kfb] twice, k3, k2tog (12 sts).

Rnds 20–24: Knit 5 rnds.

Rnd 25: [K2tog] 6 times (6 sts).

Break yarn and draw tightly through sts with tapestry needle.

Finishing

Locate the beginning of the rnds on the body (there should be a line of jogs where you switched colors)—this will be the bottom of the body. Using this as a guideline, attach buttons to front of body, spaced about 5 stripes apart from each other, using sewing needle and thread.

Slip lining into body, so that knit side of the lining faces purl side of the body. Using the long tails you left on ends of body section, attach one end of lining to body using tapestry needle and mattress stitch, adjusting for the difference in stitch count as you seam (A, above).

Note: On the purl side of the lining, slip tapestry needle under the V that appears between purl sts for each stitch.

Stuff lightly between body and lining, without over-stuffing. (The piece should look filled out, and you should be able to slip your hands inside comfortably.) Close up the opposite end in the same way as the first.

Stuff feet and attach to body using mattress stitch, with two feet on either side of the beginning-of-round line on the body, and the back two feet spaced wider apart than the front two feet (B, above).

Stuff horns and attach to top of body, placed just a little outside of eyes.

Weave in all loose ends.

FEET EATERS

These cozy critters want to gobble you up! But they realize it's more socially acceptable to keep your feet warm instead.

TECHNIQUES » Kfb, k2tog (k3tog), ssk (sssk), picking up stitches, mattress stitch

YOU'LL NEED » Worsted-weight yarn in any main color, any contrasting color, white, and black • Set of 7-inch size 8 US (5.0mm) double-pointed needles, set of 7-inch size 6 US (4.0mm) double-pointed needles • Tapestry needle • Stuffing • **Samples knit with** Cascade 220 (4/worsted weight; 100% wool; each approx 3½ oz/100g and 220 yds/201m) • 2 skeins 9478 (Cotton Candy) • 1 skein each 7808 (Purple Hyacinth), 7827 (Goldenrod), 7812 (Lagoon) • <1 skein each 8505 (White) and 8555 (Black)

FINISHED SIZE » Small [7–8 inches], (Medium [8½–9½ inches], Large [10–11 inches])

GAUGE FOR LARGER NEEDLES (SOLE AND SIDES) » 4 inches = 16 sts and 33 rows of double-stranded yarn in garter stitch (knit every row)

GAUGE FOR SMALLER NEEDLES (FACE) » 2 inches = 10 stitches and 14 rows in stockinette stitch (knit on RS, purl on WS)

> **MAKE US FOR**
> Fatigued foot soldiers

Notes: Instructions for the Sole and Sides sections include all three sizes written together, but the Face section is written separately for each size. Teeth and ears are worked the same for all sizes.

Sole (SIZES S [M, L])

With two strands of CC and larger needles, CO 6 (8, 10) sts to work straight.

Shape heel

Row 1: K1, kfb, k to last 2 sts, kfb, k1 (8, 10, 12 sts).

Row 2: Knit.

Repeat the above 2 rows twice more (12, 14, 16 sts).

Knit 16 (22, 30) rows.

Shape ball of foot

Row 1: K1, kfb, k to last 2 sts, kfb, k1 (14, 16, 18 sts).

Knit 5 rows.

Repeat the above 6 rows twice more (18, 20, 22 sts).

Knit 0 (6, 10) rows.

Shape toe

Row 1: K1, k2tog, k to last 3 sts, ssk, k1 (16, 18, 20 sts).

Knit 3 rows.

Repeat above 4 rows 3 more times (10, 12, 14 sts).

Next row: K1, [k2tog] twice, k to last 5 sts, [ssk] twice, k1 (6, 8, 10 sts).

Knit 1 row.

BO all sts.

Sides

Make a separate bobbin or small ball of about 7 yards of MC, then with two strands of MC and larger needle, pick up and knit 16 (20, 24) sts down the right edge of sole, beginning at the middle of the widest point. With a second needle, pick up and knit 6 (8, 10) sts across heel. With a third needle,

nano
KNITS

Win friends with tiny toys that can
hop in a coin purse, sit on a laptop,
or swing from your earlobes.

Human Beans

»

Micro Mountains

»

Hamster Herd

»

Petite Pencil

Plucky Mushrooms

HUMAN BEANS

Racial harmony, yum!

TECHNIQUES » Kfb, k2tog, I-cord

YOU'LL NEED » Fingering weight yarn in small amounts of skin color (Color 1), pants color (Color 2) and hair color (Color 3), plus black • Set of size 1 US (2.25mm) double-pointed needles • Tapestry needle • Stuffing • Samples knit with Koigu Premium Merino (1/super fine; 100% wool; each approx 1¾ oz/50g and 170 yds/155m) • 1150.5 (pink), 2395 (brown), 1200 (yellow), 2300 (blue), 2351 (green), 2260 (purple), and 2400 (black)

FINISHED SIZE » 1½ inches tall

GAUGE » 2 inches = 19 stitches and 23 rows in stockinette stitch (knit on RS, purl on WS)

Note: This toy is not suitable for small children.

Body
(WORKED FROM TOP DOWN)

With Color 1, CO 6 sts onto 3 needles and join in a rnd.

Rnd 1: [Kfb] 6 times (12 sts).

Rnd 2: Knit.

Rnd 3: [Kfb, k1] 6 times (18 sts).

Rnds 4–7: Knit.

Switch to Color 2.

Rnds 8–13: Knit 6 rnds.

Stuff before continuing.

Rnd 14: [K2tog, k1] 6 times (12 sts).

Separate legs

K6 on one needle, and place remaining 6 sts onto another needle to work later.

With 6 working sts, knit 3 rows of I-cord, then break yarn, leaving a long tail of about 15 inches, and draw tightly through sts with tapestry needle to finish off.

Thread tail down through leg and reattach to next st on other needle (A, opposite, top).

Knit 1 row. Next, work 3 rows of I-cord, then draw loose end tightly through sts with tapestry needle.

Arms

With Color 1, knit a 3-stitch I-cord until approx 1½ inches long, or 14 rows. Thread it straight through body with tapestry needle where the colors change.

Finishing

Close up gap between feet with one or two stitches using tapestry needle.

Embroider eyes by making two small horizontal stitches with black yarn and tapestry needle.

For hair, with Color 3 and tapestry needle, make a long, diagonal stitch across head, beginning just above one eye. Continue to make a row of these stitches until head is covered (B, opposite, bottom).

Weave in all loose ends.

A After knitting the first leg, cut the yarn and thread it down through the leg and reattach it to the next stitch to begin the second leg.

MAKE US FOR
Humans

B Embroider on hair with long, diagonal stitches across the top of the head using tapestry needle and Color 3.

MICRO MOUNTAINS

One small step for man, one even smaller mountain range.

TECHNIQUES » Backward loop cast-on, k2tog, stranded color knitting, mattress stitch

YOU'LL NEED » Fingering-weight yarn in small amounts of purple, blue, and pink (MC), off-white (CC), plus small amount of black • Set of size 1 US (2.25mm) double-pointed needles • Tapestry needle • Stuffing • Samples knit with Koigu Premium Merino (1/super fine;

100% wool; each approx 1¾ oz/50g and 170 yds/155m) • 2260 (purple), p803 (pink), 2300 (blue), 0000 (off-white), and 2400 (black)

FINISHED SIZE » Approx 1 inch tall

GAUGE » 2 inches = 19 stitches and 23 rows in stockinette stitch (knit on RS, purl on WS)

Note: This toy is not suitable for small children.

With MC, loosely CO 20 sts using backward loop method, leaving a tail for seaming. Distribute sts onto 3 needles, and join in a rnd.

Knit 6 rnds.

Rnd 7: [K3, k2tog] 4 times (16 sts).

Rnds 8 and 9: Knit.

Rnd 10: [K2MC, k2CC] 4 times.

Switch to CC only.

Rnd 11: [K2, k2tog] 4 times (12 sts).

Rnds 12–14: Knit.

Rnd 15: [K2tog] 6 times (6 sts)

Break yarn and draw tightly through sts with tapestry needle.

Finishing

Pinch CO edge closed, and seam using mattress stitch.

Embroider eyes by making two small horizontal stitches with black yarn and tapestry needle.

Weave in all loose ends.

To connect mountains together in a freestanding "range," overlap two with one slightly in front of the other and tack together. Continue to add each mountain, alternating placement in front and in back.

MAKE US FOR
Not-so-ambitious outdoorsy types

PLUCKY MUSHROOMS »

These colorful fungi are up for a good time (while they last), but bear in mind that they hate "fungi" puns.

TECHNIQUES » Kfb, k2tog

YOU'LL NEED » Fingering-weight yarn in small amounts of off-white (MC), red (CC), green, and black • Set of size 1 US (2.25mm) double-pointed needles • Stitch holder • Tapestry needle • Stuffing • **Samples knit with** Koigu Premium Merino (1/super fine; 100%

wool; each approx 1¾ oz/50g and 170 yds/155m) • 0000 (off-white), 2220 (red), 2330 (green), and 2400 (black) • 1200 (yellow) and 2351 (green) for CC alternates

FINISHED SIZE » Approx 2 inches tall

GAUGE » 2 inches = 19 stitches and 23 rows in stockinette stitch (knit on RS, purl on WS)

Note: This toy is not suitable for small children.

Mushrooms

With MC, CO 18 sts onto 3 needles and join in a rnd.

Rnds 1 and 2: Knit.

Separate for small mushroom

Rnd 3: K3, place the next 12 st on holder, k3.

Distribute the 6 working sts onto 3 needles and join in a rnd.

Rnds 4–6: Knit.

Switch to CC.

Rnd 7: [Kfb] 6 times (12 sts).

Rnd 8: [Kfb, k1] 6 times (18 sts).

Rnds 9 and 10: Knit.

Rnd 11: [K2tog, k4] 3 times (15 sts).

Rnd 12: Knit.

Rnd 13: [K2tog, k3] 3 times (12 sts).

Rnd 14: [K2tog] 6 times (6 sts).

Insert a small amount of stuffing into top of small mushroom.

Break yarn and draw tightly through sts using tapestry needle.

Form large mushroom

Place 12 sts from holder onto 3 needles, reattach MC to last st, and join in a rnd.

Rnds 15–24: Knit 10 rnds.

Switch to CC, and place marker.

Rnd 25: [Kfb] 12 times (24 sts).

Even rnds 26–40: Knit 15 rnds.

Rnd 27: [Kfb, k1] 12 times (36 sts).

Rnd 29: [Kfb, k2] 12 times (48 sts).

Rnd 31: Knit.

Rnd 33: [K2tog, k6] 6 times (42 sts).

Rnd 35: [K2tog, k5] 6 times (36 sts).

MAKE US FOR
Fungis? Fun...girls?

Using a tapestry needle, attach the grass to the base of the mushrooms, making stitches of varying lengths.

Rnd 37: [K2tog, k4] 6 times (30 sts).

Rnd 39: [K2tog, k3] 6 times (24 sts).

Rnd 41: [K2tog, k2] 6 times (18 sts).

Rnd 42: [K2tog, k1] 6 times (12 sts).

Stuff mushroom top, and break yarn and draw tightly through sts with tapestry needle.

Grass

With green yarn, CO 4 sts onto one needle to work straight, leaving a long tail for seaming.

Row 1: [Kfb] 4 times (8 sts).

Row 2 and all even rows: Purl.

Row 3: K1, [kfb] twice, k2, [kfb] twice, k1 (12 sts).

Row 5: Knit.

Row 7: K1, [k2tog] twice, k2, [k2tog] twice, k1 (8 sts).

Row 9: [K2tog] 4 times (4 sts).

BO all sts on purl side.

Finishing

Stuff stem of large large mushroom through the opening at bottom.

Close up gap between two mushrooms (where you separated for the small mushroom) with a few small sts.

Line up edges of grass with the CO edge of mushrooms, with the knit side of the grass facing down. With tapestry needle, sew tail attached to grass to mushrooms using stitches of differing lengths to give it a "grassy" effect (above, left).

With black yarn and tapestry needle, embroider eyes, with one small stitch each for the small mushroom and two stitches each for the bigger mushroom.

Weave in all loose ends.

HAMSTER HERD

So quick to make, they'll multiply faster than the real thing.

TECHNIQUES » Kfb, k2tog, I-cord
YOU'LL NEED » Fingering weight yarn in small amounts of brown and gray, plus black • Set of size 1 US (2.25 mm) double-pointed needles • Tapestry needle • Stuffing • Samples knit with Koigu Premium Merino (1/super fine; 100% wool; each approx 1¾ oz/50g and 170 yds/155m) • 2395 (brown), 2392 (gray), and 2400 (black)
FINISHED SIZE » 1¼ inches long
GAUGE » 2 inches = 19 stitches and 23 rows in stockinette stitch (knit on RS, purl on WS)

Note: This toy is not suitable for small children.

Body (WORKED BACK TO FRONT)

CO 6 sts onto 3 needles and join in a rnd.

Rnd 1: [Kfb] 6 times (12 sts).

Rnd 2: [Kfb, k2] 4 times (16 sts).

Rnd 3: Knit.

Rnd 4: [Kfb, k3] 4 times (20 sts).

Rnds 5–9: Knit 5 rnds.

Rnd 10: [K3, k2tog] 4 times (16 sts).

Rnds 11 and 12: Knit.

Stuff before continuing.

Rnd 13: [K2, k2tog] 4 times (12 sts)

Rnd 14: Knit.

Rnd 15: [K2tog] 6 times (6 sts).

Break yarn and draw tightly through sts with tapestry needle.

Ears and Tail

Cut a 20-inch-long strand of yarn, and with tapestry needle, wrap yarn around 1½ sts near front of body about 5 or 6 times until it puffs out (A, right). Thread loose end back into body, and repeat for second ear, spaced about 4 stitches from the first. Do the same to make a tail, wrapping a stitch directly above the CO opening.

A To make an ear, wrap yarn around 1½ stitches using yarn and a tapestry needle.

MAKE US FOR
Cute addicts and their enablers

B Thread one I-cord through the bottom of the body from back to front.

C Pull the I-cord through to form one front and one back foot, then repeat for the other front and back foot.

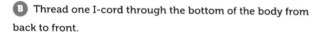

Feet (MAKE 2)

CO 2 sts onto one needle, and knit an I-cord until approx 1 inch long. Thread it back to front through bottom of body to form one front and one back leg (B and C, above).

Repeat for other leg.

Finishing

Embroider eyes by making two small horizontal stitches with black yarn and tapestry needle, placed just in front of ears.

Weave in all loose ends.

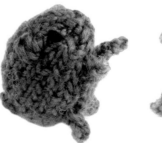

PETITE PENCIL

There's never a dull moment with this humble No.2.

TECHNIQUES » Kfb, k2tog

YOU'LL NEED » Fingering weight yarn in small amounts of pink (Color 1), gray (Color 2), yellow (Color 3), tan (Color 4), and black (Color 5) • Set of size 1 US (2.25mm) double-pointed needles • Tapestry needle • Stuffing • **Samples knit with** Koigu Premium Merino (1/super fine; 100% wool; each approx 1¾ oz/50g and 170 yds/155m) • 1150.5 (pink), 2392 (gray), 1200 (yellow), 2360 (tan), and 2400 (black)

FINISHED SIZE » Approx 2½ inches long

GAUGE » 2 inches = 19 stitches and 23 rows in stockinette stitch (knit on RS, purl on WS)

Note: This toy is not suitable for small children.

With Color 1, CO 4 sts onto one needle.

Rnd 1 (work as I-cord): [Kfb] 4 times (8 sts).

Distribute sts onto 3 needles, place marker, and join in a rnd.

Rnd 2: [Kfb] 8 times (16 sts).

Rnds 3–5: Knit.

Switch to Color 2.

Rnds 6–8: Knit.

Switch to Color 3.

Rnds 9–22: Knit 14 rnds.

Rnd 23: [K1 Color 4, k1 Color 3] to end.

Switch to Color 4 only.

Rnds 24 and 25: Knit.

Rnd 26: [K2tog, k2] 4 times (12 sts).

Rnd 27: Knit.

Stuff before continuing.

Rnd 28: [K2tog, k1] 4 times (8 sts).

Place sts onto one needle to work as I-cord, and switch to Color 5.

Rnd 30: [K2tog] 4 times (4 sts).

Rnd 31: Knit.

Break yarn and draw tightly through sts with tapestry needle.

Finishing

Weave in all loose ends. Embroider eyes with two small horizontal stitches in black yarn.

MAKE ME FOR
Victims of writer's block

DESIGN YOUR OWN KNITTED TOY

Once you've knit a few patterns from this book, you may be saying, "I could invent some way better toys." Prove it by actually doing it!

1. Sketch It

Start with a sketch of your toy design. It's a good idea to sketch it from two different angles so that you have a good idea of the finished shape you want.

I'll use the pig from Pigs with Wigs as an example here because it's representative of the kind of designs I usually create.

2. Divide It

Divide your sketch into its most basic shapes. These can include tubes, spheres, and flat pieces. Shapes that align perpendicularly to adjacent shapes (as in legs to the body) will be separate pieces. Shapes that look like they grow out of other shapes (as in the pig's snout to its body) can probably be knit as one piece.

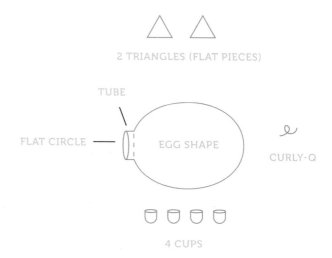

2 TRIANGLES (FLAT PIECES)

TUBE

FLAT CIRCLE —

EGG SHAPE

CURLY-Q

4 CUPS

SIDE VIEW

FRONT VIEW

3. Plan It

Now that you know what pieces you will knit, you can roughly plan how you will knit them. Because decreases have a smoother appearance than increases, I usually begin knitting at the back or bottom of a toy (where I'll use increases) and knit to the top or front of the toy (where I'll use decreases).

For perpendicular arms and other appendages, I start knitting at the part that will be attached to the body and knit outward.

To make your toy three-dimensional, you'll next determine what kinds of increases and decreases to use in your pieces. You can sketch these as lines or "seams" on your toys.

To simplify this, let's work with just the body of the pig. To get an elongated "egg" shape for the pig's body, I begin by increasing 6 evenly spaced stitches every other round, then when the pig is as wide as I want, I knit some rounds without increases or decreases before decreasing for the front of the pig.

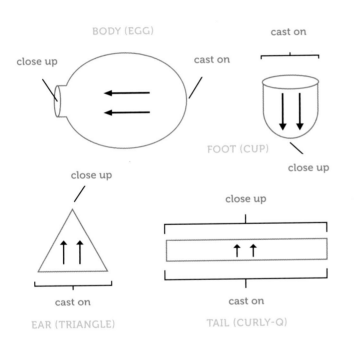

BODY (EGG)

close up

cast on

cast on

FOOT (CUP)

close up

close up

EAR (TRIANGLE)

cast on

close up

cast on

TAIL (CURLY-Q)

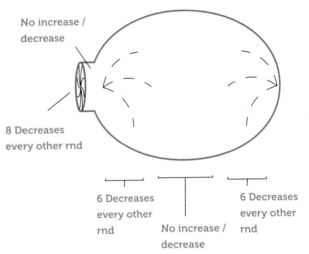

No increase / decrease

8 Decreases every other rnd

6 Decreases every other rnd

No increase / decrease

6 Decreases every other rnd

BASIC KNITTED SHAPES

Here are some basic guidelines for how many increases to use to create different three-dimensional shapes. Knitting without increases or decreases gives you a straight tube. Evenly spaced increases every other round make your piece grow outward in all directions.

TUBE
No increases

FLAT CIRCLE
8 evenly-spaced increases every other round

ROUND SHAPE
6 evenly-spaced increases every other round

ELONGATED ROUND SHAPE
4 evenly-spaced increases every other round

4. Number It

Before you jump right into knitting, decide if you need to do any math to make your design work out well.

In the case of the pig, I have two considerations in deciding how many stitches to cast on. First, I want the hole to be as small as possible, and second, because I increase by 6 stitches in the first round, I need a multiple of 6. The number 6 is the smallest multiple of 6, so 6 it is!

After I increase and decrease with multiples of 6 stitches, I want to decrease 8 stitches every other round for the flat part of the snout, so the stitch count by the time that I get to the beginning of the "tube" of the snout should be a multiple of both 6 and 8. I think 24 stitches is a good number to use.

Then, I close up the body with a multiple of 8 stitches (and like the cast-on end, a smaller number is best for closing up), so I make a note to close up with 8 stitches.

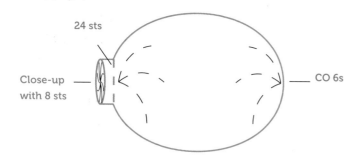

24 sts

Close-up with 8 sts

CO 6s

If you know that you want a particular size toy, you can knit a swatch for gauge and calculate exactly how many stitches you want to have on your needles at different points. (See the section on gauge on page 00.) Or you can just start knitting and see where your needles take you!

5. Knit It

Instead of trying to map out the entire pattern before knitting it, I prefer to begin knitting at this point, using the guidelines I set up in the previous step to help me along.

To keep track of what I'm doing, I type short notes on my computer as I knit. For example:

CO 6 sts

[kfb] 6 times

knit every other rnd

next rnd: [kfb, k1] 6 times

etc. until 60 sts . . .

6. Check It

Once you have made some progress, take a step back and see if there is anything you want to change. Is your toy too small, or too big? I find it helpful to stuff the piece so that I can see what shape it is taking, then remove the stuffing before continuing to knit.

If you don't like what you see, backtrack a bit and try something else—for me, this often means changing the frequency of my increase/decrease rounds or changing how many increases or decreases I use in a single row. The world will not end if you have to rip out part or all of your toy and try something different!

TIP: When I go back and change something about a design, I make sure to save the notes that I took for my previous version as a reference.

7. Continue It

When you are happy with your progress, it's time to think about how you want to shape the rest of your toy. Look back to your sketches for guidance, then continue knitting and checking your progress.

For the pig, when the piece becomes as wide as I want, I begin to knit without increases or decreases to elongate the shape.

When the piece is about half as long as I want the finished body to be, I make a note of how many rounds I've knit without increases or decreases, and knit the same number of rounds. Then I begin decreasing every other round until I end up with 24 stitches as I had planned.

Again, I stuff it to see how it looks.

As I planned in my sketches, I knit without increases

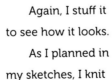

or decreases to get a tube shape for the snout before decreasing to finish off with the flat circle.

Finally, we have a piggy shape!

How do you like your completed piece? If it's not quite what you hoped for, go back to your sketches and see if a different technique, stitch count, or shaping might produce better results. If you decide to try something drastically different, I recommend starting over with new yarn instead of ripping out the piece you just finished so that you can compare the two.

TIP: When designing a new toy, wait until you finish the entire toy and you are happy with the design before weaving in loose ends or attaching safety eyes. That way, you can take pieces apart if necessary.

8. Appendage It

Now that you have a body, you have to give it legs, arms, wings, or anything else that it wants! My process for designing these appendages is similar to that for the main body piece, except that because these pieces are much smaller, I use more trial and error and less math and mapping out.

For example, I know that I want to use simple, two-

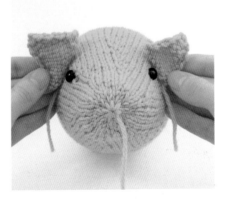

dimensional triangular pieces for the pig's ears, so I experiment with making a few ears in different sizes and shapes before I settle on a design that looks the best when held up against the body.

The ear on the left is a little big, but the ear on the right is just right!

9. Finish It

When you have assembled all the pieces and you love what you see, then you can attach eyes, weave in all the loose ends, and embellish with embroidery.

To me, less is more in terms of style. That's why I use small safety eyes and just two simple embroidery stitches for the pig's nostrils.

10. Write It and Share It!

Once you have a design that you're happy with, go back to your notes and re-type them in a clear and more detailed way. You may find it helpful to refer to the patterns in this book for abbreviations and other pattern conventions.

It's a good idea to remake your toy from your written pattern to be sure that you wrote down everything correctly and you are happy with the techniques you used. That way you know that you can make the same toy again at any time without having to do the design work again.

If you want to share your pattern with the world, whether through a blog or another format, it's a great idea to have someone else to test out the pattern by knitting it. I've found that enlisting a few knitters with various skill levels helps to ensure that any mistakes or unclear parts are caught before I publish.

Seeing your design come to life in another knitter's hands is immensely exciting and satisfying, so I encourage you to give it a try!

KNITTING ESSENTIALS

BASIC STITCHES

I recommend starting out by learning to knit with two needles, then switching to double-pointed needles (see page 20) once you feel comfortable with the basics.

Casting On (CO)

The most common way to start a knitting project, unless directions specify otherwise, is with a long-tail cast-on.

Based on the number of stitches to cast on, estimate how much of a tail you will need. For me, with worsted-weight yarn and size 5 US (3.75mm) or 6 US (4.0mm) needles, I use about 10 inches per 10 stitches, or 1 inch per stitch.

If you are leaving an extra length for seaming, add another 10 inches or so to the tail.

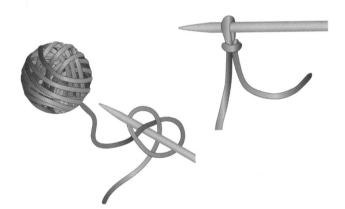

1 Make a slip knot with the yarn, slide the needle through the knot, and tighten. This will become the first stitch in the cast-on.

2 Grasp both yarn ends in your left hand, with the yarn attached to the ball around the outside of your thumb and the tail around the outside of your forefinger.

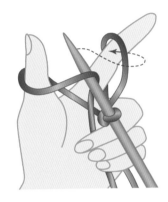

3 With the needle in your right hand, insert the tip of the needle under the outer side of the yarn on your thumb, then dip it over and round the inner side of the yarn on your finger.

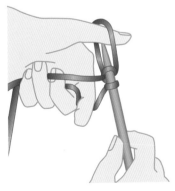

4 Let the yarn slip off your thumb, and pull outward slightly on the stitch you just made to tighten the loop on the needle. Repeat Steps 2–4, trying to cast on all your stitches with the same tension, until you have the required number of stitches on your needle.

The knit stitch is the most basic stitch.

1 Hold the needle with the stitches in your left hand, with the yarn attached to the rightmost stitch. Hold the empty needle in your right hand. (In circular knitting, the attached yarn will be on a different needle—see "Using Double-Pointed Needles" on page 20.) Insert the tip of the right needle under the front of the first stitch on the left needle.

2 Wrap the yarn around the tip of the needle in your right hand, wrapping on top of the needle, from left to right.

3 Pull the right needle back out through the stitch on the left needle, pulling the wrapped yarn out with it.

4 Slip the stitch off the left needle. You now have a new stitch on the right needle.

Repeat Steps 1–4 as many times as indicated in the pattern, or until you have transferred all of the stitches from the left needle to the right.

When you come to the end of the row:

If you are knitting a flat piece with two needles, switch the right needle to your left hand and flip it around for the next row.

If you are knitting with double-pointed needles, keep the right needle in the same position and move on to knit from the next needle that follows in the round.

The Purl Stitch (P)

The purl stitch is the reverse of the knit stitch—it happens automatically on the reverse side of knitted stitches. When knitting a flat piece, you flip the piece around to work purl stitches on the reverse side.

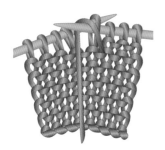

1 Insert the tip of the right needle under the front of the first stitch on the left needle, going in from the right side and coming out in front of the left needle. Wrap the yarn around the top of the needle, from right to left.

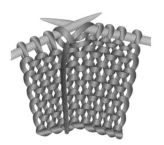

2 Pull the right needle back out through the stitch the left needle, pulling the wrapped yarn out with it.

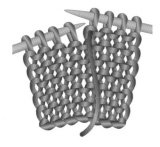

3 As you pull the needle and yarn through, slip the stitch off the left needle.

Repeat these three steps as many times as indicated in the pattern, or until you have transferred all of the stitches from the left needle to the right.

Binding Off (BO)

Most of the three-dimensional pieces in this book end with instructions to draw a loose end of yarn through the stitches to close off. For flat pieces, however, the usual finishing technique is to bind off stitches.

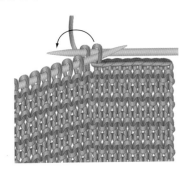

1 Knit the first 2 stitches in the row as you normally would. Slip the left needle into the first stitch you knit, and pull it over the second stitch and completely off the needle. One stitch is bound off.

2 Knit the next stitch in the row, so that you again have 2 stitches on the right needle and repeat until there are no more stitches on the left needle and you are left with only one stitch on the right needle.

3 To finish off, break the yarn, slip the stitch off the needle, and and slip the loose end through the stitch. Pull tightly to secure.

Note: If a pattern calls for you to bind off on the purl side of a piece, you will bind off in the same way as described above, except that you will purl all stitches instead of knitting them.

INCREASE AND DECREASE STITCHES

You need increase and decrease stitches to knit more than a rectangle or a straight tube—like some curves!

Knit through Front and Back of a Stitch (kfb)

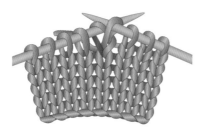

1 Knit a stitch just as you normally would, but without pulling the stitch off the left needle.

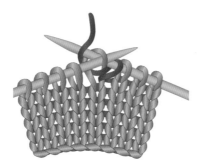

2 Knit into the same stitch again, this time inserting the tip of the right needle through the back leg of the stitch. Once you pull the right needle and yarn through, slip the left stitch off the needle.

This will increase the total number of stitches by 1.

Knit 2 Together (k2tog)

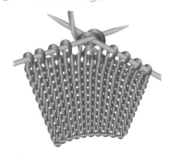

Insert the right needle under the first two stitches on the left needle. Wrap the yarn as you would normally do for a knit stitch, and slip both stitches off the left needle.

This will decrease 1 stitch.

Slip, Slip, Knit Together (ssk)

1 Insert the tip of the right needle through the front of a stitch as if to knit, then slip the stitch off the left needle without knitting.

2 Repeat for the next stitch on the left needle.

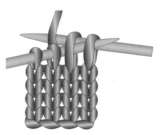

3 Insert the left needle through the front of both slipped stitches on the right needle, and knit together.

This will decrease the total number of stitches by 1.

Purl 2 Together (p2tog)

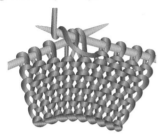

Insert the tip of the right needle purl-wise through the front of the first 2 stitches on the left needle.

Wrap the yarn around, pull it through, and slip both stitches off the left needle.

This will decrease the total number of stitches by 1.

Knit 3 Together (k3tog)

Insert the tip of the right needle knit-wise through the front of the first three stitches on the left needle. Wrap the yarn around, pull the yarn through, then slip all three stitches off the left needle. This will decrease the total number of stitches by 2.

Slip 3, Knit Together (sssk)

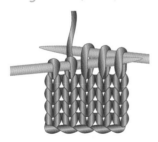

Slip 3 stitches knit-wise from the left to the right needle. Insert the tip of the left needle through the front of all 3 stitches on the right needle, and knit together. This will decrease the total number of stitches by 2.

BEYOND BASICS

Some extra techniques will help you create the wonderful creatures in this book.

Backward Loop Cast-On

This is an alternative cast-on technique that gives you a less bulky starting edge. It can also be used in the middle of a piece to add additional stitches.

1 Hold the needle in your right hand. Hold the end of the yarn attached to the ball in your left hand, and loop it around your thumb.

2 Insert the tip of the needle under the yarn on the outside of your thumb.

3 Let the yarn on your thumb slip off, and tighten the stitch by pulling gently on it.

Repeat Steps 1–3 until you have cast on the specified number of stitches.

Provisional Cast-On

A provisional cast-on, made with a crochet hook, will allow you to go back to your first row of stitches and knit them in the opposite direction. Use waste yarn of a similar weight but a different color from your knitting yarn.

1 Make a slip knot and place it on the crochet hook. With the hook in your right hand and the knitting needle in your left, bring the yarn behind the needle and to the front above it.

2 Catch the yarn with the hook and pull through to form a chain—you have made one stitch.

3 Repeat until you have the number of stitches called for on the needle, then continue to make a few more chain stitches using the crochet hook only. Cut the waste yarn and gently pull out the last loop in the chain to secure.

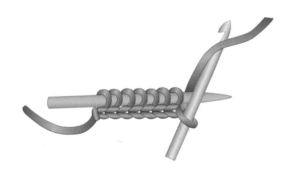

Later in the pattern, you will undo the waste yarn so that you can knit from the other direction.

With the piece held right side up, with the waste yarn at bottom, undo the knot in the waste yarn on the right side, and gently pull the waste yarn to "unzip" it. As the stitches come out, slip a needle under each one to catch it.

I-cord

An I-cord is a small tube of circular knitting made using two double-pointed needles.

Slide the stitches down the needle in your left hand so that the stitch without the yarn attached is on the right side. Knit the first stitch with the yarn that is connected to the last stitch, pulling the yarn around the back of the needle. Continue to knit to the end of the row.

When you reach the end of the row, instead of turning to work the other side, again slide the stitches down the needle and knit the first stitch with the yarn that is connected to the last stitch.

Yarn Over (yo)

Yarn over is an increase stitch that makes a small hole in your knitting.

1 Bring the yarn around in front of the needle in your right hand.

2 Knit the following stitch as you normally would, wrapping the yarn around the needle in the back.

Knitting Essentials

Picking up Stitches on a Flat Piece

Picking up stitches along the side of a finished piece will allow you to knit in another direction, and in the case of toy knitting, it will help you to add another dimension to your knitting. (Some toy patterns call for stitches to be picked up in the middle of a 3-dimensional piece. See page 39 for this technique.)

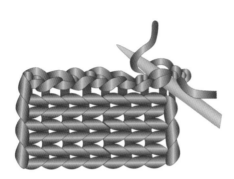

With the piece turned sideways, insert the tip of the needle under the first side stitch. Wrap the yarn around as you would for a knit stitch, and pull the yarn out through the stitch.

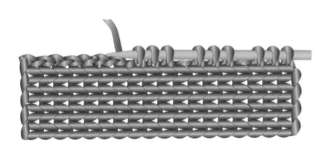

Repeat across the side of the piece, adjusting for the difference between the number of side stitches and the number of stitches to be picked up by skipping every fourth or fifth side stitch.

Joining a New Ball of Yarn or a New Color

To join a new ball of yarn to one that will run out soon, tie the end of the working yarn and the end of the new ball together in a loose knot. Knit one stitch with the new yarn, then pull the knot tighter and closer to the back or wrong side of the piece.

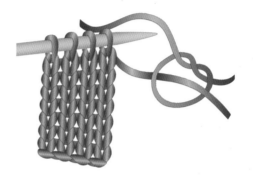

Use this technique when a pattern calls for you to switch to a new yarn color, and you won't be using the first color again (or not again for many rows).

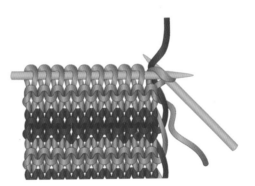

If you will use the first color again soon, as in a striped piece of alternating colors, do not tie a knot or cut the yarn, but instead carry the first color loosely up the side or back of the piece until you will use it again.

Stranded Color Knitting

Stranded color knitting (or Fair Isle, as it's also known) is a method of carrying multiple strands of different colors of yarn along the back of a piece as you knit, incorporating the different colors in your stitches as you need them. Often, there will be a chart to refer to for the color changes.

You want to keep a consistent, relatively loose gauge, without pulling any stitches too tight, so that the finished piece doesn't pucker.

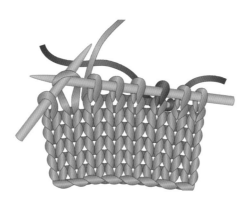

As you knit, you can either hold the two strands of color in different hands, or you can simply drop the color that you're not working with at the moment (my preferred method). Wrap the colors of yarn around each other every few stitches to secure the yarn not being used.

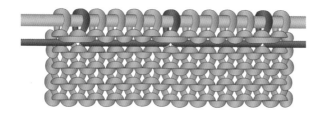

Looking at the back of the piece, you should see the two strands of yarn, smooth and not puckered, across the entire length of a row.

Picking up a Dropped Stitch

Dropped stitches happen to the best of us. If you notice that your stitch count is off, you may have a "run" in your knitting, where one stitch has fallen off the needle, and a vertical row of stitches has unraveled along with it.

Instead of ripping out the entire piece and starting over, insert a crochet hook through the bottommost stitch that is still in place, then hook the bar that lies directly above it. Pull the bar through the stitch, then repeat for every bar above until you reach the topmost row of stitches. All fixed!

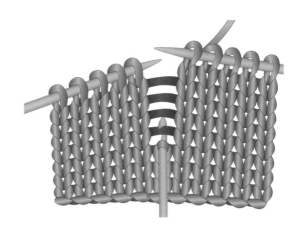

HOW TO READ CHARTS

Most knitting patterns use written instructions to guide you in knitting a project. In some cases, though, a chart is the best way to convey a design with more complex stitches or color patterns.

A few patterns in this book incorporate charts for some pieces or sections. The charts are either for flat knitting or repeated patterns for circular knitting.

Both flat and circular charts are read from the bottom up and have some row/round numbers indicated as guides. On both types of charts, one square equals one stitch, and at least one complete pattern repeat is shown in the chart.

A chart for flat knitting indicates right and wrong side rows. Right side rows are read right to left and wrong side rows are read left to right, just as you work the stitches in the pattern. The key that appears along with the chart will often tell you to interpret the same symbol one way on a right side row and another way on the wrong side row.

MC (knit on RS purl on WS)

CC (knit on RS purl on WS)

8

8 total rows

Read Row 2 and all even rows left to right

Read Row 1 and all odd rows right to left

1

8 total stitches

A chart for circular knitting represents a color or stitch pattern that is repeated a given number of times for every round, and it can also indicate repetitions of rows.

Because you always work stitches right to left in circular knitting, every round is read from right to left in a chart for circular knitting. And because you are always knitting on the right side of a piece, the key that appears with the chart doesn't mention wrong side rows.

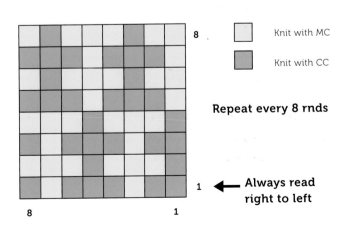

8

Knit with MC

Knit with CC

Repeat every 8 rnds

1

Always read right to left

8   1

Repeat every 8 sts in rnd

KNITTING ABBREVIATIONS

Here is a list of abbreviations used in the patterns in this book.

<	Less than
]	Repeat actions in brackets number as many times as specified
approx	Approximately
BO	Bind off
CO	Cast on
est	Established
k	Knit
k2tog	Knit 2 stitches together
k3tog	Knit 3 stitches together
kfb	Knit through front and back of one stitch
p	Purl
p2tog	Purl 2 stitches together
rnd(s)	Round(s)
RS	Right side
st(s)	Stitch(es)
St st	Stockinette stitch (knit on right side, purl on wrong side)
ssk	Slip 2 stitches to right needle and then knit them together
sssk	Slip 3 stitches to right needle and then knit them together
tbl	Through back loop
WS	Wrong side
yo	Yarn over

METRIC CONVERSION CHART

INCHES TO CM		CM TO INCHES			
1/16	0.16	1	3/8	36	14 1/8
1/8	0.32	2	3/4	37	14 5/8
3/16	0.48	3	1 1/8	38	15
1/4	0.64	4	1 5/8	39	15 3/8
5/16	0.79	5	2	40	15 3/4
3/8	0.95	6	2 3/8	41	16 1/8
7/16	1.11	7	2 3/4	42	16 1/2
1/2	1.27	8	3 1/8	43	16 7/8
9/16	1.43	9	3 1/2	44	17 1/4
5/8	1.59	10	4	45	17 3/4
11/16	1.75	11	4 3/8	46	18 1/8
3/4	1.91	12	4 3/4	47	18 1/2
13/16	2.06	13	5 1/8	48	18 7/8
7/8	2.22	14	5 1/2	49	19 1/4
15/16	2.38	15	5 7/8	50	19 5/8
1	2.54	16	6 1/4		
2	5.08	17	6 3/4		
3	7.65	18	7 1/8		
4	10.16	19	7 1/2		
5	12.70	20	7 7/8		
6	15.24	21	8 1/4		
7	17.78	22	8 5/8		
8	20.32	23	9		
9	22.66	24	9 1/2		
10	25.40	25	9 7/8		
11	27.94	26	10 1/4		
12	30.48	27	10 5/8		
13	33.02	28	11		
14	35.56	29	11 3/8		
15	38.10	30	11 7/8		
16	40.64	31	12 1/4		
17	43.18	32	12 5/8		
18	45.72	33	13		
19	48.26	34	13 3/8		
20	50.80	35	13 3/4		